Over the Side, Mickey

Over the Side, Mickey

A sealer's first hand account of the Newfoundland Seal Hunt

Michael Dwyer

Nimbus Publishing Limited
PO Box 9301, Station A
Halifax, NS B3K 5N5
(902) 455-4286

Design: Margaret Issenman
Cover photo of seals by Dr. Wayne Lynch; cover photo of Michael Dwyer by Bruce Lee.

Printed and bound in Canada.

Canadian Cataloguing in Publication Data
Dwyer, Michael, 1953-
Over the side, Mickey
ISBN 1-55109-253-0
1. Sealing — Newfoundland. 2. Dwyer, Michael, 1953- I. Title.
SH362.D97 1998 639.2'9'09718 C98-950156-6

Nimbus Publishing acknowledges the financial support of the Canada Council and the Department of Canadian Heritage.

To the memory of my father Captain Leo Dwyer,
who spent his life at sea and instilled in me the values of
honesty, hard work, and family.

Monday, April 7

Like birds of a feather, sealing and misery stick together. It started again for me at 4:30 P.M. that evening, an hour after we slipped the lines off the wharf in Twillingate. Battening down while cruising on the fringes of the "Big Pond," I felt the first tell-tale signs of oncoming seasickness: hot beads of sweat formed on my forehead and my throat contracted involuntarily, more and more frequently. I was huddled in the lee of the superstructure on the exposed aft deck of the *C. Michelle*, a sixty-foot long-liner, owned and operated by Perry, a forty-nine-year-old skipper from my home town.

The southern edge of the immense arctic ice pack was reported to be thirty miles offshore, three and one-half hours' steam through a moderate three-metre ground swell. Burning bile built in my throat; my eyes watered. The revulsion I felt from the smell of frying bologna mixed with diesel fumes confirmed that my misery had begun. Staggering to the rail with the roll of the hull, my stomach yelled, "Reject!" and I vomited over the side into the surging foam. I clung tightly to the rail, helpless to the throes of nature that convulsed my body a dozen times before I got a chance to gulp in a lung full of crisp, sobering air and wipe the scalding tears from my eyes and face. Frigid spray lashed me.

I heard someone say, "Mick is sick! Hold on tight, don't fall overboard," as I watched, through blurred eyes, the foam surge past, at times inches from my nose. I was miserable. The cold, twenty-five-knot wind solidified the sweat as it popped from my pores and it charged inside my coat, attacking my vitals. Ice crystals as hard as stones stung my exposed face, but I didn't care. They seemed to be doing me more good than harm.

The door to the superstructure opened. Gerard came out on deck. "You all right?" he asked, zipping up his coat and looking around, smirking all the while.

"What do you think?" I replied, turning from the foam. Standing with my back to the superstructure, sheltered from the cut of the wind, clinging onto the hot hydraulic pipes protruding through the wall, swaying back and forth, side to side, pitching and rolling to the rhythm of the sea, I tried to straighten up. Breathing deeply, I wiped away the water streaming down my face, trying hard not to look at him. I was really glad when he swayed aft to check the bindings that lashed down the speedboat. A gust of wind brought another cloud of oily, black smoke and my guts revolted again. As I lunged for the rail, a tortured groan escaped from my burning throat. "Oh God! This has got to be the worst!"

Gerard, satisfied that the speedboat was secured, returned to the lee, and after I had straightened up again, together we watched the ice-glazed head of Twillingate Long Point get swallowed up by the swells. A shiver coarsed through my body and I shook uncontrollably until it had passed.

"Do up your coat before you freeze," he said.

Not having the energy to do up the zipper, I was content to stay as I was, clutching the hot pipes, at one with the rolling ship. I didn't feel really cold. Shifting to stand right in front of me, Gerard reached for the zipper and zipped up my coat. Unable to hold back any longer, with me looking him in the face, he burst out laughing.

"Don't laugh, Gerard," I said, with as much seriousness as I could muster, only to hear him bellow out in laughter again. "It's not funny!" He was forty-four years old, six months younger than me. He had worked aboard for eight years and was generally looked upon as the mate. He was single, but he maintained a home, and cared for his two aging parents. I had sailed with him last spring to the Hunt. He was his usual steady, kind, considerate, example-setting self. He had seen me this way before, clinging to the rail of a lurching long-liner, with frigid foam flowing at eight knots ten inches from my freezing nose.

"All up yet?" he asked, as I molded myself against the swaying wall again, a long, drawn-out, "ooohhh!" escaping my lips.

"I think that's the last of my dinner," I croaked. I wiped my eyes with the back of my hand and looked around. Everything was rolling or pitching, rising and falling, all at once. Long Point had disappeared; there was nothing steady in sight. The penetrating wind bit me, making me aware of how cold it was. Squeezing all my muscles tight and holding onto the warm pipes, I sweated and shivered all at once.

"Come in the warm," Gerard said, reaching to open the door. "You're going to freeze out here."

"I'll be there in a minute," I groaned, my eyes closed, hardly able to stand up straight. "I'll be all right."

He closed only the bottom half of the metal, watertight door, and a blast of heat washed over my face. I was cold and seasick and it wasn't the first time. I suffered this misery every time I sailed after being "land-lubbering" for a few months. It was a purging. I remembered back over half my lifetime ago, sailing with my father loaded with railway tracks from Halifax, Nova Scotia, bound for Houston, Texas. The first eight days out at sea: eight days seasick, everything coming up, and nothing staying down. It had taken eight pounds off my one hundred and thirty-pound frame.

"Ha, ha, you got it going there now," I heard a voice say. It was David in the doorway. Glaring at him through scalding eyes, I saw him root a piece of bologna from between his teeth and study it intensely, before slowly swallowing it with an exaggerated movement of his Adam's apple. My glare, diluted by my tears, became a wince at the thought of bologna, and I urged myself away from him back to the rail.

"Get it up! Puke it up!" he said to my back, as another half-dozen convulsions racked my spent body. "When you get that dark, brown taste in your mouth, force yourself to stop because that'll be your rectum. Don't spit that away," he laughed.

I veered from the rail towards him, but he disappeared inside before I got within arms' reach. I grabbed the pipes instead, gasping in fresh, blasting, arctic air, wishing I were dead. "Oh God!"

The bitter cold drove me inside fifteen minutes and a small bottle of bile later. I knew I'd freeze if I stayed out there any longer. The head was located first door, starboard side, and three feet up the narrow companion-way. Swaggering inside, I struck the heat and the smells of the interior. This, combined with the roll of the boat, made me frantic to get the door open. Randy, another strapping seal hunter, stood in the galley doorway, port side, eight feet further along. He was thirty-three years old, 190 pounds, and married with two teenaged children. He spied me before I could get inside.

"You all right?" he asked, as I tried to get through the opening, my throat constricting with an oncoming glutch. "My God, you're some white!"

"No," I replied, trying to focus my eyes on the far wall and the toilet. Making heavy contact with the door box, banging my shoulder, my face grimacing in pain, I pulled myself hastily inside the small room, firmly closing the door behind me. Towels swung back and forth on the hooks. Charging my way to the sink, I turned on the hot water to wet my facecloth.

Hot steam enveloped my bowed head; the heat from it quelled the nausea. Spitting what I hoped was the last bit of bitter bile into the mist, I pushed myself partially upright with the rolling sequence of the sea, glad to see that mist coated the mirror. I certainly wasn't going to use my reserves to wipe it away to look at myself. I knew how I looked because I knew how I felt and I felt the sight of me would make me even sicker. Instead, I grabbed for my facecloth and burned my hand with the scalding water. I whipped my hand away. At that precise instant, the boat rolled, hurtling me across the tiny room. The square, wooden, outside edge of the shower stall saved me, at the cost of my elbow. I winced in pain and held on with my good arm as the hull lurched violently the opposite way, trying to throw me back. Waiting for the right time, I staggered back to the steaming sink, groaning all the way. Turning on the cold water, moaning a long, lingering, agonizing lament, I put the wet cloth to my splitting forehead and sat carefully back upon the throne. I was feeling rotten and I knew I looked like crap. Lifelessly, I unzipped my coat to let some heat down inside to quell the shivers.

"Are you all right?" a voice asked through the door.

"No. I'm far from all right," I groaned, holding my throbbing head in my hands, swaying back and forth on the toilet. "But I am still alive, thanks."

"You sure?" the voice came again. I recognized it as Darrell's. A wiry, twenty-two-year-old, 160 pounds, married, with one small child, Darrell had just bought a new house and truck. He was David's younger brother and has worked the *C. Michelle* for the longest period of time, next to the skipper.

"Yes," I replied.

"The kettle is boiled. Come have a hot cup of tea." I heard him say something else as he walked away, but I didn't hear him laugh.

Brushing my teeth was my next step to recovery. Opening the vanity doors, I reached for my shaving kit containing my toothbrush. The relief was immediate. I felt the worst was over, and I might save some of my morning's breakfast. Brushing away, I was relieved to find that the thought of bologna didn't make me retch. Replenishing the brush with paste, I let the minty water drain freely from my mouth, watching it slosh back and forth in the sink. I rewashed my face, took off my coat, and sat back down.

I was a pathetic excuse for a sealer. Wallowing lifelessly from side to side like the colored towels, my chin rested on my chest, my burned hand rubbing my injured elbow, groaning in unison with the swells. Unconsciously, I timed them. Seven seconds from crest to three-metre crest. "Crest," I thought. I brushed my teeth again.

Knowing I couldn't stay there forever, I summoned my strength to go to the galley for tea. I knew the next step to recovery from the curse of sickness was to fill up my stomach with something solid (chewing it up really well so it wouldn't scrape my throat on the way back up) and try to keep it down for ten to twelve hours. If this failed, "repeat as required." "Crackers and tea," I thought. Letting out a deep sigh, I waited for the right time to cautiously stand up and stagger to the door.

Randy watched me hang my coat in the closet and slide to the door. Trying really hard not to look at him, I ricocheted up the hall, focusing my attention on the doorway. Sheepishly brushing by him, I heard him say, "Make room for him to sit down, boys."

The galley was not a spacious place; the refrigerator, the cupboards, and the stove took up half of it. The rest was eating space, with a table and two bench seats. Most of the crew was swaying around, sitting, standing, eating and passing the time.

Darrell got up for me to sit down. I shifted in next to David and Darrell slid in beside me. He looked at me for a moment, holding back his chuckle, his eyes glinting. "Your misery hasn't started yet, I see," I said, trying to glare at him.

"No, not yet, but I got a feeling it's not very far away," he replied, bursting out laughing, along with Paul and Rodney, swaying back and forth on the other side of the narrow table.

Paul was twenty-eight and the biggest crewman. He was single, but saving to buy a new house anyway. He was an inshore fisherman, fishing with his brother from open boats for crab, lobster and other species he was allowed to catch.

Rodney was the skipper's son, a wiry twenty-two-year-old, recently married. Having a skipper's ticket, he captained the *C. Michelle* on trips that Perry took off to remain ashore.

"You'll get your share of it before this is over," I said, as Randy placed a mug filled with steaming hot tea on the table in front of me. As I reached across for the milk, the cabin lurched. My elbow struck the mug, upsetting it all over my lap. David and Darrell sprang away from me. Rodney stopped the mug, but not before my lap absorbed the scalding water. I tried really hard not to swear. There was nothing I could do, nowhere I could lunge, I just absorbed it. My body, still shrunken with cold, dissipated the heat quickly, leaving me just wet. Randy passed in another steaming cupful saying, "Drink this one, Mick." Through their chuckles, Darrell added sugar and milk to my groaned instructions. Carefully I reached for a few crackers while Randy slid the wet paper towels off the table.

As I was putting one to my mouth, I heard Rodney say, "Pass me in a can of sardines, Randy, please." I took a bite of the cracker, hearing the cupboard door close. I chewed away and tried not to look at the tin can on the table next to me. My first sip of hot tea burned my lips and the inside of my mouth. I spit it all out in my paper napkin. Everyone tried to keep from laughing. I pulled away from the cup, putting my napkin to my mouth, clunking my injured elbow on the table. I felt like crying. I looked at them. We all had tears in our eyes. I strained to suppress a howl that would have scared the living daylights out of every seal for fifty miles. I had to get control! Only two hours into the Hunt, I was a pathetic wreck already.

Rodney hooked the key into the sardine can. Nonchalantly, he rolled back the lid. Everyone seemed to become suddenly interested in the movie blaring out from the TV. Looking out the window, over Paul's right shoulder, I became distinctly aware of the taste of bile and toothpaste mixed with tea in my mouth and I felt a small bead of sweat form on my forehead. I concentrated on the thought, "Crackers and tea."

I bit into the biscuit trying to ignore the sardines, drowned in oil, that lay exposed on the table. I despairingly chewed and chewed. "Cracker. Cracker." I thought. "Paul, could you crack that window a little?" I asked, swaying towards Darrell.

"No problem," he said with a grin, opening it half way. A frigid blast of swirling wind brought the pungent, sickening smell of sardines to my nostrils. Dropping my head forward into the steam of my tea, I swallowed down the soggy mouthful, all too conscious of Rodney sticking his fingers into the can. The greasy fish held my gaze and I watched it drop into his mouth and disappear inside. He chewed in long, exaggerated motions. I put the rest of my cracker into my mouth and scrunched it up, thinking, "so it doesn't scrape my throat." He reached for sardine number two.

I couldn't help but watch the revolting process. Grease smeared his fingers and he licked them clean. The taste of warm tea turned to hot bile and I knew the purging was peaking again. I fought against the first unpreventable convulsion that shook me. Darrell knew and he made room for me to escape. Randy handed me a coat as I barged past him, heading for the open deck. The closing door cut off the words, "Hold on tight." Wind attacked me and the lurch of the hull hurled me foreward. Totally oblivious to the danger, I almost went overboard. With a great effort I pulled my face from the surging foam and certain death. Frightened and relieved to still be aboard, I moved back away from the gunnel and grasped the hydraulic lines for dear life. Rather than fall in the icy sea, I decided to hold on and let it all go from there. I knew there'd be a lot more repulsive things than a bit of bile on that deck before this expedition was over. Besides, at that point, I couldn't have cared less.

Clutching the warm lines, my life support system, I watched nature take her course. Grey sky, grey sea, icy water surrounding me. Winds that cut right through my bones, hurtling ice hard as stones. Everything was in motion. Plunging into the troughs, everything around me was liquid violence. The smaller, foam-lathered wind-waves atop the powerful, rolling swells looked to me like dirty, bared teeth. On the crests, I saw miles and miles of them. There was nothing steady to be seen. "Ice-rubble" speckled the froth, some pieces as large as me, some smaller. They fell away astern, playing "peek-a-boo" with me in the swells. A dozen seagulls trailed us, watching our wake. They seemed to laugh, smirk and make fun of me, squawking amongst themselves.

"You'll get no more from me." I said out loud.

The top half of the door came open. "Here's your tea. It will warm up your guts," Darrell said with a grin.

"My guts are evenly spread out over the last ten nautical miles," I replied, taking the mug from him. He laughed and pulled his naked arm back inside. A waft of heat licked me and I again realized I was freezing. The tea warmed me a little and I began to feel better, breathing in the cold, salty air, constricting my muscles against the shivers.

"Come in out of the cold?"

"I'm coming in now," I replied, molding myself against the wall, swaying lifelessly with the ship, shivering and sipping tea. It revived me and gave me something besides bile to spit at the foam. The biting winds cooled my lungs and I started feeling better. I took in a deep breath and expelled it completely, immediately taking in another. I lifted my heavy head and tried to balance it on my drooping shoulders, focusing my watering eyes on the shifting deck, telling myself that it was all up, that that was the last of it. That thought resuscitated me to the point where I figured it was time to go inside. Lunging down grade towards the door, I had a vague feeling that my "sea-legs" were returning.

Feeling more balanced and attached, I fluidly hung my coat in the closet and entered the head. The taste of toothpaste and the feel of warm water on my throbbing head brought me around. Without incident, I left the bathroom and ricochetted up the companionway to the three steps leading up onto the bridge, giving Randy the mug and saying nothing. On the starboard side, Perry sat in the captain's chair, practically surrounded by electronic equipment: radios, a compass, GPS, depth sounders, fish-finders, radars and other equipment necessary to find and capture sea creatures. "Sick, are ya?" he asked, swiveling around in the chair to look at me. I noticed a big grin on his face.

Clutching the console for some sense of stability, not wanting to look at him, I replied, "Yes sir, sicker than a gut-shot dog hood."

"We'll be making the ice in an hour or so, things will simmer down then."

"It don't make any difference. I've got to go through this every time, anyway. It's a purging process I never escape when I go back on the sea after being ashore for a spell. It's penance for something I must have done on land." He seemed to get a great chuckle out of that.

"Sins will be paid in full, one way or the other," he said, turning his attention back to the instrument panel. I was glad he did. Icy sea water attacked the windows three times every single minute. Not really feeling up to seeing the view for a prolonged period, I turned towards the entrance to the forecastle.

Rodney occupied the only other chair available—the rumble seat. He was stretched out with his feet on the top of the chart-table. He pulled them back as I made my advance and stretched them out again after I passed. Saying nothing more, I paused at the entrance for the right timing, turned around and backed down the ladder into the close confines of the tiny forecastle.

With the motion of the boat, I cautiously descended the eight oak threads and stood on the small triangle-shaped, canvas-covered floor. It was stuffy and hot. A low rumble thundered through my head. My kit bag was among six others piled in a heap against the carpeted bulkhead, where seven rifles hung in a floor-to-ceiling rack. Sweaters and coats swung there as well, swaying back and forth, back and forth. Needing a change of clothes, I had to move three or four luggage bags to get my own. Bending over and focusing caused a sickening reaction within my racked body. I grabbed at the blurred handle, spun around and plopped down atop the pile, staring at the floor, completely resigned to the torture, lifelessly swaying in unison with the clothes.

"You don't look so good," I heard Gerard say from the lower bunk. Glaring at him through scalding tears, I groaned, "Tell me something I don't know." The walls of my lower stomach slammed together. "Oh God help me."

Gerard shifted in his berth and passed me a piece of gum. I accepted, fumbled with the wrapper and dropped it on the floor. I couldn't look down for it and I knew I couldn't move to get it, so I forgot about it, closing my eyes. Concentrating on my breathing, barely audible over the sound of water rushing by the hull, I heard Gerard say, "Want me to get you on the video?"

Not even bothering to open my eyes or lift my head, I didn't reply. I couldn't. I was a lifeless lump of luggage, swaying on the swells of misery and I couldn't help it.

A lifetime later, it seemed, the feeling of pain aroused me and I awoke to the dead weight of Darrell's boot crushing my toes. Startled,

I automatically struck out at his leg to push him off. "Sorry about that," he said, surprised by my reaction. "I didn't see you there."

"I'm not here really," I snapped, wrapping my sore arms about my bent legs and squeezing myself into a ball. "My body, such as it is, is here, that's all. The rest of me is gone." Resuming the "despair position," I was vaguely aware of him as he whipped off his sweater and crawled into his berth in the bow, as fluid as a cat.

The small forecastle contained seven bunks: three port side, four starboard. The remaining room consisted of lockers, crammed full of supplies. The middle bunk port side was packed with clothes, bags, and rifle cases. My bunk was middle, starboard side, and I had the urge to crawl in and die quietly, but I knew I couldn't muster the energy to move. It hurt to lift my head. Finding some degree of contentment in the fact that the convulsions had passed, I remained where I was, groaning my despair aloud.

"Take off some clothes and crawl in your bunk," I heard Gerard say. I didn't move. I thought I heard him snicker just before I dove into a welcome state of despondency.

Thump! I awoke to the violent shifting of the hull. We had entered the ice fields. *Thump*! The boat careened off another pan and I heard the crunch of ice along the hull. "It's started now," Gerard said, getting up. "Forget peace and quiet from here on in," he added, heading up the ladder. I lolled on the floor rolling with the punches, a totally useless piece of meat. It was 6:30 P.M. *Thump! Crash! Crunch! Smash! Bang! Crash! Thump! Lurch! Reel!*

The words, "Never again!" resounded inside my heavy, aching head. "Nothing is worth this part of it. Nothing! How much is this worth an hour?" Gordie Lightfoot's words swam through my swirling mind: *Does anyone know where the love of God goes, when the waves turns the minute to hours..?*

What was an even more revolting thought was knowing, deep in what was left of my guts, the fact that the misery had hardly started. After seasickness, if we were really lucky, came endless hours on the open, exposed deck, in an arctic abattoir. I knew it was going to get a lot more miserable than this. The roar of scrunching along the hull froze the mental image. Tightening the hold I had around myself, I groaned in despair at the thought.

We hoped for four hundred seals a day. To first find, then retrieve, butcher, pelt, decapitate, wash, scrub, clean and stow on deck overnight to cool, before being lifted, shifted, dragged, lifted, tossed, separated, moved, stowed, counted, iced and secured in the hold first thing the following morning. We hoped most of them would be young harps weighing sixty to eighty pounds.

Mature harps were fair game; they were included in the quota. We'd be killing the old males. Weighing four hundred pounds, they were larger and more aggressive than the females, and it wasn't unusual to pluck one from a pan, leaving his harem of two or three healthy females looking at us in a surprised, defensive, "on-the-edge-of-the-pan" posture. We'd harvest as few of them as possible. They were more revolting to butcher because during the sculpting process, milk spilled out. When this mixed in with the gallons of steaming blood, the smell was pungent and the sight of it was enough to spill your guts. The general rule was, "if you kill a bitch, you clean the bitch!"

Thump! "Jumpin', skipper, you're gonna hole 'er!" I heard Darrell roar. Trying to lift my head and focus my eyes, I saw him scramble out of his bunk and, holding on, pull on his sweater in tune with the pitch of the tiny cabin. I felt my head strike the side of the solid oak ladder, at rung number four, just before I had time to catch myself. *Whack!* Stars exploded around me and I let out a yelp in reaction to the pain I felt. I dared not let go for fear that the next impact would throw me back the other way. Clutching the ladder, I held on, absorbed the pain, and braced myself.

"You won't live there, my son!" Darrell stated, straightening out his homespun sweater. "I'm helping you up out of that."

I tried to help him lift me but failed. It didn't seem to make a lot of difference. He plucked me from the floor and gave me handholds to Randy's top bunk. I tried to thank him but couldn't—my mouth was dry. I tried to swallow instead. A congealed lump in my throat stretched a bit and sprang solidly back into place. "What, did you wet yourself?" he grinned, looking down at my crotch.

Pathetically, I lifted my head to his ear in an effort to spew out the word, "Tea." *Crash!* Like a rag doll I was thrown against him. He didn't move; it was like being molded to a rock. The momentum whiplashed through my body, through my stiff and aching neck, smacking my forehead solidly against his bony shoulder.

"You're having a hard old time of it, skipper," I heard him say, an intense wave of unadulterated pain shooting through my limp body.

I tried to ask, "What was your first clue?" but I couldn't. Nothing worked, nothing responded. My deadened brain roared at me, "Straighten up!" so I started from the floor. Before long I was swaying solo, one hand holding on, the other rubbing my aching head. Darrell eased up on his support and focusing on my pillow I took a few deep breaths.

Darrell slipped a piece of gum into my mouth. "Here, chew on this." The relief was instant. "No trouble to put the headlock on you, now," he laughed, and tossed the wrapper into the swinging refuse bag. "You'll be all right." Reaching for the ladder, he grinned at me.

"Yes," I surprised myself to be able to say, "I'll be the best kind. I'm going to change my clothes and go out for fresh air. If I'm not up in five minutes, I'll give you permission to release me from this misery with my own rifle, there on the rack."

"I'm not the gunner," he chuckled, starting up the ladder. "You'll have to get someone else to do that. In the meantime, hold on with at least one hand and try to land as softly as you can." Then, quick as a wink, he was gone, leaving me alone in the ricochet room.

The more I chewed the better I felt. I noticed the rolls of the hull got longer and slower, indicating our progression through the pack; the greater the distance from the weathered edge the weaker the swells became, except in severe storms when the awesome power of the sea paraded for miles and miles into the ice-field. After extracting what I needed from my kitbag, I peeled off my clothing, accessing the burn on my lap, happy to find that my most valued personal possession had escaped injury. I eased on clean clothes.

The engine reduced its thrust and I felt the hull scrunch to a halt, gently rocking back and forth. I used this lull to finish dressing and, without incident, wearily climbed the ladder to the bridge.

It was still bright evening, I noticed, squinting through the windows. As my eyes adjusted, I realized it was not all that bright. Actually it was dismal for 7 P.M. Randy sat in the rumble seat; Rodney slouched in the captain's chair. All I craved was fresh air, and I knew where to get plenty of that. I made my way directly to the closet, and retrieving my heavy winter coat, fur hat and scarf, I wrapped them all around me. Twisting the frost-covered handle, I opened the door and stepped out into the freezer.

It was neither stuffy nor congested on deck. For as far as I could see it was dismal grey. The ice had us completely surrounded. To the horizon, the crust shifted and lifted, rose and fell, wheeled and crunched. These were the floes, our foes.

They were intimidating. The two-foot-thick pans were multi-layered, frozen together in distorted and haphazard patterns, shapes, forms, angles, and directions. Glowing sour-milk-white beneath the surface, some seemed to be reaching for the rudder. They spoke loud and clear of high pressures, powerful seas, and freezing temperatures—a rough place to eke out a living.

Ice pinnacles, ten to twenty feet high, fragments of pressure-ridges, were scattered randomly throughout the pack. Like posted sentries, they jostled among themselves with the toss of the sea, trying to get a better look at me. All of it—hundreds of millions of tons of ice—rose and fell effortlessly all around me. The immense ice-field made its own shroud of cold mist that stuck to my face, sending shivers racing through me. This was my workplace.

My father's words as he seized my hand at the rail of the *Gulf Star*, just before the start of my first Hunt, twenty-eight springs before, drifted through my mind: "Be careful son. It's either you or the ice." A thunderous blast from the horn had split the crisp dawn and resounded across the floes, to signal the start of what was then "The Greatest Hunt in the World."

"I'll be all right, dad," I said. "Butterflies will keep me light, adrenaline will keep me quick, and prayers will keep me safe." Sliding my hand out from beneath his, I abandoned the rail and joined in the slaughter that was in full "swing" at very close quarters.

Back to reality, I gasped in another lung full of crispy air and pulled my coat zipper all the way up. Most of the crew were atop the wheel-house. Deciding to go up, I stepped up on the fish-hold cover, grasped the steel ladder, and climbed the eight rungs to the top deck.

My cooler was strapped to the railing nearby, and opening it, I took out a bag of candy barrels. Placing one in each cheek, I felt the "double barrel" rejuvenation effect immediately. They both split down the middle shortly after my third suck.

"What do you have there?" I heard Gerard ask, after I kneed the cover of the cooler closed.

"Life-savers," I responded with a rushing swallow of relief. I handed him the bag and looked around. Miles and miles of nothing but ice, like the swirled topping of a gigantic cream pie with small lakes of gun-metal blue water interlacing the cream. I heard someone above me cough, and looking up twenty feet in the rigging, amid the antennae and guy-wires I saw Perry and Paul standing. Paul looked frozen to death. From where I stood, it was hard for me to distinguish where his red survival suit hood stopped and his face began. "Want a candy?" I called to him.

"Yes, and a hot cup of tea," was his reply. Cautiously turning around he climbed down. Gerard handed him the candy bag.

"How long were you up there?" I asked, taking the bag and putting it in my pocket, thinking how much his face reminded me of a cooked lobster.

"Two hours," he replied, as his body went into an uncontrolled shiver. "Feels like two weeks. I'm going for coffee now, before anything else. If you need me, I'll be in the galley." His survival suit cracked every step of the way.

Perry had another look around before he came down. He scanned the massive ice-field with binoculars, looking for the least hazardous path. There was no path to be seen through my watering eyes.

Everything was shifting and white. I figured it was fifteen below zero on the aft deck, twenty-five below in the lee of the control booth where I huddled and at least forty below in the rigging. The western horizon seemed crisper in the glow of the setting sun, from which the wind whipped through me, unabated, at twenty-five, gusting to thirty-five marrow-freezing knots. The long-liner, purring in neutral, lolled back and forth.

Perry, agile as a cat, climbed down, shook himself violently a few times in front of me to get his blood circulating, and stated, "Seems to be a bit slacker to the northeast. I'm going to work my way up through for the rest of twilight and we'll burn down for the night. We're clear of the wharf, that's the main thing, isn't it, boy?" He took off his glasses, wiped eye-water from his fleshy cheeks, and shook himself inside his insulated coveralls.

We had spent the three previous days tied up to the wharf waiting for a break in the low-pressure system that had settled over the northeast coast for a week. It was late to be starting the Hunt. This time last spring, we had been on our second trip. Everyone was getting a little stir-crazy lying around, eating, passing the time while nearly two hundred ships cracked it to the herd. Perry had showed his true colours one morning when David took out a pound of bacon to fry up with some eggs. The bacon was on the counter when he came into the galley, picked it up and put it back in the freezer, saying, "There's no need of eating that. You're not doing anything!"

After he went out, David exclaimed to one in particular, "We're paying for the food and not allowed to eat it! Don't that beat all." But we ate our eggs without bacon that morning.

"Sounds good to me, Skipper," I replied, trying to avoid his stare. Really, I didn't care. Getting us in the fat was his department.

"How are you feeling, now?" he asked, wiping his glasses with a paper towel he fished from his pocket.

"I'm getting better all the time. I hope the purging is over."

"That's good," he said, fumbling to put on his glasses. "It's almost better to be blind then wear this nuisance of a thing!" Turning away, he went inside the control booth, where he operated the joystick controls for the rudder, with rudder indicator on the left, throttle and transmission controls on the right. As he opened the throttle, a thick cloud of oily-black smoke spewed from the stacks. The fumes engulfed me and I spun around, the smell making my stomach retch, screaming; "Reject!" My mouth filled with soggy crackers and sweat broke out on my face. The wind whisked the sickening smoke away. Looking at Gerard standing at the gunning table on the port side, eight feet from the booth where I huddled, I gagged and said, "Holy smokes Gerard! What are we burning? Coal?"

"Oily bows," he replied. Walking up beside him, I held onto the spar guy-wire, tightening my body against the brunt of the wind, watching the frosting crunch slowly by. To punch our way through the seemingly inpenetrable white, Perry turned and aimed the bow, adjusting the throttle as necessity dictated. Every now and then, a sunken pan surfaced around the blades, causing a chewing vibration throughout the hull. At this sound, he'd shift into neutral and wait for the shuddering to stop. Then, shifting to half ahead, we'd continue our battle. Each time the Volvo roared, the smoke poured. Knowing I'd be sick again if I stayed there in the frosty fumes, I climbed down the ladder to the aft deck.

The only water to be seen from there was the pathetic wake, which foamed up frosty white, specked with chunks of ice, stretching back fifty yards or more before the floes gobbled it up. The gulls were gone. Shivering, I thought of where they were perched for the night; on an ice-pan somewhere, standing on one leg. I knew I'd have it better than that.

"Come in for a mug of tea." Turning, I spotted Paul leaning out the galley window. "It'll put some lead in your pencil," he said, with a wind-burned grin.

"I need more air. Besides, one thing I don't need out here is lead."

"I'll pass you out a mug of hot tea," he said. "How do you take it?"

"You look good and chipper. I'll have it the way you have yours."

"Comin' right up," he said, withdrawing into the galley. Two minutes later, the hot liquid was bringing me around somewhat.

The air was fresh and sobering. I sensed the curse abating. I could even distinguish some beauty in my shifting, frozen surroundings, seeing the form of a bird in a clump of ice. Its spread wings of translucent-blue balanced precariously, bobbing and swaying with the motion of the sea, as if it was just pitching for the night. The engine quieted to idle; work was done for the day.

Randy was out on the forward deck. Paul jumped out on a large raftered pan and Randy fed him slack rope as he circled a few high clumpers before passing the end back to him. He fed out another thirty fathoms and made fast to our mooring for the night. Gerard came over beside me. "You're looking better now."

"I feel better, too. I'm over it for now. A lunch and my sleeping bag, in that order," I said. "I'm sick of this day."

"My plans are the same."

Perry was coming down off the roof for the final time that day. He shook himself a few times before disappearing inside behind Gerard. A few seconds later the Volvo shut down. The sounds of the ice pack engulfed me completely. It was all-encompassing. The swiler rocked slowly in the swells, alternately; the ice nibbled up one side, then the other. The wind was dying out. It was a peaceful time in the floes. A pan nudged the hull, sending a shiver from stem to stern as if to remind me that I had better not forget the fact that it was all subject to change without notice in a bitter short time. The North Atlantic was one of the most inhospitable places in the world without the ice. We weren't very deep into the floes. The wreck of the *Titanic* wasn't that far from here.

Listening, I couldn't hear any harps bawling. They were reported twenty-five miles to the northeast. We might be closer to them this time tomorrow night. Anyway, enough conditioning for one day. Thinking of the gulls, I reached for the frosty door handle, glad to be able to close out the arctic night and go inside in the warm.

The thing about being cold and miserable is the immediate, almost overpowering sense of rejuvenation one feels as things improve. "Aaahhh!" Heat and comfort lifted me as I took off my scarf, hat, coat, and boots and stowed them away. Then I felt hunger.

Darrell shifted out for me to sit in as I made way with another steaming mug of tea. I got seated without mishap and proceeded to eat an apple, a bowl of cereal, and two slices of homemade bread with jam. The crew was watching *Batman* on TV. I glanced at it as I ate, saying nothing, relishing it all, happy to be in the warmth, not sick and not out there.

"Feeling a lot better now, eh?" Darrell inquired.

"Yes, thank you," I replied, looking straight at him. "Another slice of bread and a few more crackers and I'll be almost back to abnormal." He burst out laughing and so did I.

Shortly after that my pillow beckoned me and I didn't resist the call. Batman, in his entire splendor, was on the screen as I shifted out. Randy, sitting across the table, asked, "What would Batman be like sealing, I wonder?"

"He wouldn't last a 'bat-watch' out here. You'd have to 'bat' him to put him out of his misery," I replied.

"More in distress makes misery the less," he quoted, tightening the lid on the jam bottle. "As far as I'm concerned, the more the merrier."

"I can't argue with that," I said, drying my utensils and putting them away. I left the galley as Batman, to the delight of all the viewers, flitted in to rescue a very attractive young lady.

The skipper was in his chair on the bridge; Rodney lounged in the other. The radar screen blipped out the shape and distance of three big bergs within a twelve-mile range, the radio emitted the news of the day as the voices of the sealing skippers boomed in loud and clear, sometimes quite candid and descriptive in their transmissions.

"The god-damned weather, it won't let up! Not fit for an old bitch hood to pup…"

"Yes, you're right b'y," a voice came back. "Worst in years. Hardly got a hundred today…if the wind veered a few points to the southwest, we might get a few seals, over."

"Back, yes, that's right, boy. No let-up in the forecast. Easterly tomorrow…thirty to thirty-five, rain…nothing is going to crawl up into that weather, over."

"Back, yes, you're right, b'y...no let-up; no change up. Large patch of seals east of Fogo...five or six boats doing very good...three and four hundred each today...over."

"Radio seals," Rodney said, pulling back his feet as I turned in the direction of the forecastle. "They fly by the thousands every night."

"Yes, I know." I turned my back on the stairwell, "We're looking for 'real seals.' " Placing my foot on the first riser, I waited for the right timing.

"It won't be tomorrow," he said.

"Tomorrow, tomorrow. If tomorrow comes," I said. "Have yourself a comfortable night's sleep."

Thump! A floe struck the starboard bow, sending a shudder through the hull. "From the sound of that, I don't think anyone will." Grasping the ladder firmly, I left him sitting in the chair. Switching on the light and holding onto my bunk, I straightened out my sleeping bag and fluffed my pillow. *Thump!* Another nudge.

The reading light in Gerald's berth was lit; he was reading a book. "Forget sleep if that don't stop," he said, turning a page. "That's worse than Randy's snoring."

"It reminds me of Beethoven's Fifth," I said, cautiously pulling off my sweater and T-shirt, hanging it on a hook. "Death banging to get in."

"If it gets in, death is a definite possibility. It's like the old fellow said, "You don't die in the floes, you perish."

A cold shiver passed through me. I peeled off my socks and joggers, eager for the warmth and comfort I knew was to be found within the confines of my sleeping bag.

Grasping the wooden frame of Randy's upper bunk, I cautiously placed my right foot on Paul's bottom rail. The next action was similar to getting up on an operating table. I lifted my body horizontally and placed my left leg inside my opened sleeping bag, feeling the comfort. Shifting most of my weight to my sore right arm, I stretched horizontally to manoeuvre in. My exposed backbone scraped along the outside wooden frame just before the manoeuvre ended and I adjusted to make the last shift. Pushing off from Paul's bunk, lifting and shifting with effort, I was in. A great sigh of relief escaped me as I settled back. Lifting my head to adjust my pillow, I banged my forehead on the plyboard bottom of Randy's bunk, not four inches from my nose. I grimaced and gritted my teeth to suppress a howl. The soft pillow against the back of my sore neck absorbed a good deal of the spasm. All that escaped my clenched jaws was an agonizing moan. David came down the ladder.

"You got it good there, now," he said to me, whipping off his shirt. "Just like the robin in the nest."

"More like a baby in the cradle," I groaned, rubbing water from my cheeks.

"Look boys, he's crying for his mommy. Ha, ha, what a pretty sight to see," he chirped, shucking his sneakers.

I was in no position to argue and I really didn't care. I pulled the warm material against my neck and turned in, only to find the move was impossible. There wasn't enough room to turn over. "Not enough room here in this tomb to change my mind," I thought, peeling the warm flap from my shoulders, turning my sore body in and covering them again before closing my eyes. I was aware of David slipping into his bunk, settling in and straightening out, without incident, without pain. I envied him and turned out my light.

Thump! Beethoven was still there, that time six inches from my nose. Instinctively shifting back from the hull, I tried to think of things other than the *Titanic.* Could I hear *The Wreck of the Edmund Fitzgerald,* leaking from David's headphones? I drew up into a tight ball and let the sandman claim me at 10:00 P.M., twenty-eight nautical miles northeast of Twillingate Long Point.

I was vaguely aware of Paul and Randy turning in sometime later and the sound of ice grating against the hull. It was then that I became acutely aware of the total blackness. Claustrophobia crawled into my subconscious. I'd suffered the symptoms of that curse since I was a little boy, pinned to the ground by my older brother, unable to move, unable to scream, unable to utter the word "uncle." Dark, confined spaces have sparked it off ever since. I looked around for some light to get myself oriented.

There was none. Placing my hands right next to my face, I couldn't see them. I touched my nose and still couldn't see them. "Not good."

Poking my head out of my bunk, I strained my eyes to detect some light. Nothing. Pulling back in, I fumbled to find the switch for my light. Fumbling and groping for it, I was aware of my breath breaking up and sweat forming on my forehead. Then, I felt it, pressed it, and the light glared on. I breathed a sigh of relief. Settling down, I looked around the tiny cubicle. Everyone else was asleep.

"I'll leave it on," I thought, "no problem then." Lying back, basked in light, I drifted back to sleep.

Tuesday, April 8

At 6 A.M. the Volvo snarled to life, signalling the start of the day. Fourteen hours of punching ice would mean punishment for both ship and crew.

Five minutes later, the hull surged ahead and the first impact of the day shook the hull from stem to stern. The nibbling sound of ice changed into a loud, crashing crescendo that filled the small cabin. "Just as well get up!" Gerard exclaimed, crawling out of his bunk, balancing himself on the lurching floor. "No more comfort here." With extreme agility, between the violent crashes and bangs he pulled on his pants, socks, shirt, and shoes and disappeared up the ladder.

I lay there in my bunk feeling the long-liner assault the floes. The continuous collisions to both port and starboard bows caused me to vibrate in my bunk. The zigzag coarse we took shifted me about and I had to brace myself against the impacts to keep from banging around too much. As the hull struck a pan right next to my ear, the crunching sound sent shivers up my spine. A mental image of clouds, of black smoke, rain, wind, and bitter cold drifted through my groggy mind.

My stomach felt tight and bothersome as if it had caved in on itself. It was empty. Trying not to think of the purging, I understood why. My head ached and, feeling my forehead, I located the bump. My shoulder hurt when I moved it and my lap was raw. My elbow was tender but other than that, I was in good shape, almost ready to face the day. Almost. I pulled my sleeping bag about my shoulders and closed my tired eyes.

Bang! My whole body, all 135 pounds of it, was lashed against the bunk. My bent knees were first to strike the solid wood framing, followed fluidly by my sore shoulder. As the pain peaked, I thought I saw the blue, jagged teeth of the pan in my bunk with me. It was my pillow. *Bang!* She struck again, this time the hull brought up solidly. My sleeping bag and I slid up against the light.

The impact roused Darrell from his lair and he came out of it growling like a polar bear. "This is it for the rest of it! Shake, Rattle, and roll! The cursed ice!" He used the relatively quiet time it took for the engine to reverse and go astern to scramble on his jeans, sweater and socks. The hull shivered and rumbled and the prop chewed ice. As the boat surged ahead again, with a pronounced lurch to starboard, he was dressed but for one sneaker. I watched him clutch it in one hand, holding on with the other, waiting. After reeling from the impact and subsequent lurch that he knew was coming, he slipped the sneaker over his foot and disappeared up the ladder saying something about a "demolition derby."

Gerard was right. There was no comfort. A pan struck just below me, in line with Paul. His reaction to the shock was the same as Darrell's: get out and get dressed quickly. That left only David, Randy, and me. Both of them occupied roomier, upper bunks. Neither one of them were asleep.

By the way we were cruising along without the grating sound I figured we had made an open lake of water. The welcome sound of water swooshed past the hull as it swayed port to starboard and we rumbled through the rubble at about five knots. Then the Volvo's quickened throb reduced abruptly, followed by the mother-of-all-*Thumps*!, endorsed with a violent lurch to port.

My sleeping bag and I slid against the wooden frame with the pitch. My bad arm passed over my body and whipped through the air, my injured elbow straightening out completely with a sickening "snap," intermingled with the sounds of shifting clothes bags. I immediately pulled my arm back to my chest and rubbed it tenderly, moaning quietly and swearing emphatically to myself. "God help me! How much is this worth?"

I suffered another dozen collisions before I was forced to surrender my berth to escape the beating. "Timing is everything," I thought, as I cautiously dressed. Randy tossed around and grumbled a bit but he made no motions to leave his place. David chose to take the beating face down, his pillow wrapped over his head like a helmet, clinging onto the outside of the wooden bunk with one knee fused to frame, rolling with the punches.

The prop chewed into a piece of ice and the hull scrunched to a halt. I took the opportunity to finish dressing and climbed the ladder into the wheel-house. The battle of ice versus hull continued.

The bridge was dull and gloomy, a direct reflection of the world outside the windows. Every pane of glass was blurred with rain and pecks of ice streamed down, their watery paths redirected by the gusts of wind that ceaselessly lashed them. I realized that I felt just as glum inside.

"Top of the morning to you," Paul said cheerfully, pulling back his legs for me to pass.

"Such as it is," I said, leaning on the chart table to get a better look around. Gerard was in the captain's chair, holding on, checking the monitors and punching buttons.

"How are you feeling this morning?" he asked.

"About the same as the weather" I replied, holding on, looking out all the windows to see ice and sleet rising, ice and sleet falling, ice and sleet swirling, ice and sleet whirling all around. Visibility was about two glum miles.

"That bad, eh?" Gerard replied, studying the coordinates on the GPS. "We drifted eleven miles south during the night. It will take us close to dinner time to regain the ground we lost."

"Go ahead, Gerard, make my day," I replied.

"No worries about seals at this rate," Paul interjected. "By the time we get there, all the seals will be killed."

"In the meantime," Gerard said, "the skipper wants lookout

posted in the spar for one hour watches. You're up in five minutes."

"I'm having something to eat first! I can't survive an hour in the friggin' riggin' on an empty stomach."

"Drink a couple of cups of anti-freeze, my son, and put some hard bread in your pocket, and don't waste time about it," he said, drawing back from me in the chair.

"You're kidding me, aren't you?" I said pathetically, turning to Paul who was grinning from ear to ear, enjoying it all.

"Yes boy, he's only funning with you. It's true about the watch. Darrell is up there now, then me, Gerard, then you. Your freezing begins at nine."

"I've got to eat something," I said, heading to the washroom, leaving them to the bleak of the bridge. I got a fright when I looked in the mirror. What a sight! I looked ten years older. The purging had taken its toll. My bloodshot eyes surveyed my gauntly face. I wasn't pleased. "Death warmed over."

The shuddering of the hull wasn't as intense here. I brushed my teeth, combed out my tangled hair and beard and gave a sigh of relief. I felt and looked a little better. As I cleaned up after myself, my thoughts were on breakfast.

I managed to pour tea and cereal without any trouble. Opening the fridge, I extracted a container of juice. Gulping down a glassful quickly, I poured another. Bread and tea swelled my shrunken stomach. David came in and slid in beside me. "Did you find your mommy last night?" he ribbed.

I shifted in a little to give room but he took a lot more then he needed. "Poor, little sick boy, crying for his mommy," he said ruffling up my hair.

"Get away from me, punk," I said.

He went to the cupboard for a mug, cutting off bread and fishing the bologna out of the fridge. "I need some air," I said, shifting from the table, knowing I wasn't ready for the aroma of bologna yet. Placing the mug and utensils in the sink, I left him alone in the galley grumbling something about the "cursed ice." I pulled on my outside clothes and went out on deck to meet the arctic morn.

It was raw. My first instinct was to compress and I turned my back to the biting winds, pulled up zippers, snapped the buttons, and stretched my woollen stocking-cap down over my ears. Rain stung my face as I made my way to the speedboat. Surveying the top deck, I saw Perry standing in the booth; Darrell was up in the rigging. His head was hunched between his shoulders, the only shelter he had from the thirty-five to forty-five knots of cutting winds. Shivering, I watched him stiffly hold on as each impact shook the hull.

From where I was, I could see no easy way through the floes. The only water I saw was in the wake, a snake of green on a vast canvas of white, worming its way left and right. Black smoke billowed from the stacks, smudging the wild grey sky. Ice pans crunched slowly by and everything was shrouded in rain and mist, fog and drizzle.

At 9 A.M. Rodney spelled Perry in the booth, Gerard relieved Paul in the spar. The floes were reluctant to let us pass; frequently we had to back up to butt our way through. Progress was slow. We had advanced only three miles since 6 A.M.

After a "last" hot cup of tea, I prepared for the rigging. Lifting the hatch to the engine room, I cautiously descended the metal ladder and stood up in the hot confines. Most of the small space was taken up by the Volvo diesel engine which worked beside me, sometimes roaring, sometimes quieting, then roaring again, all the while generating heat. It was close to one hundred degrees. Heavy outer clothing swung from hooks all around.

Carefully shifting forward, I leaned my weight against a wooden bench for support as I slipped off my shoes, the first move in the dressing gauntlet. I was wearing long underwear, jogging pants, woollen socks and a T-shirt. I pulled on a long-sleeved shirt and buttoned it up, followed by a heavier pair of woollen socks, then coveralls. My brow was wet as I straightened out my hooded sweater and hauled on insulated boots. Sweating profusely, I scrambled up the ladder to escape the stifling heat, closing the hatch cover behind me. I finished dressing in the companionway—woollen hat, scarf, gloves and heavy coat—in full realization of the fact that whatever

I wore, I was going to be frozen in fifteen minutes.

Gerard came down the spar as I climbed atop the wheel-house. He shook himself violently for half a minute before saying, "It's all yours. Hold on tight."

I started my ascent. It was gut-wrenching. When I was halfway up, thirty feet above the aft deck, a tremor shook the boat and I catapulted to port. I held on for dear life and was slammed against the spar. Horrified, thinking I was going to fall, I clung on desperately, until the shuddering stopped. Pooling all my nerve and tightening my churning guts, I cautiously continued on up and turned around, sitting for a spell on the wooden platform.

It was a precarious perch. I grasped onto an antenna and got used to the feel of the stem crashing through and bouncing off ice pans, acutely aware of the solidifying trail down my back. Below me, in the heated booth, Perry worked the controls, punching our way ahead. The ice-field stretched to the horizon. The swell was all but gone. Icy specks of rain stung my face when I looked directly into the 'lazy wind' that cut right through me rather than go around. My eyes watered and I felt what had been sweat solidify inside my shirt. Shivering, I secured a handhold further up the antennae and cautiously stood up. My heart pounded in my throat and butterflies fluttered in my stomach. It was a scary place.

Small lakes of water intermittently broke the white monotony, the closest one about a mile ahead the bow. Black smoke billowed away to the eastward, smudging the already gloomy, grey sky. The floes were heavy and rugged, making me think of the ship as an ant struggling across the surface of an enormous frozen cream pie. I saw no seals. A few ice-gulls were the only sign of life.

It was bitter cold! A squall of biting wind tore a piece out of the back of my neck and the cold surged in. Shooting down my backbone, it charged through me, using my arteries as speedways, slamming to a halt at the end of my extremities. I instinctively reached to put up my hood to stop it; it was up. Oh God! I resigned myself to it. Thinking of *Death on the Ice*, and the miseries endured by my predecessors over the course of three days and two nights, I knew an hour wouldn't kill me…chill me to the core, yes—but it wouldn't kill me.

By the time we made the open lead, my skeleton was rattling freely under my frosty clothes. Perry asked once for directions and for some reason, I crisply pointed a frozen arm towards a huge iceberg, about four miles distant. Ice grated. Even time seemed to freeze. It was about then that I began to wonder why I was up here. It all looked the same and at this rate, it would take until dawn to get to the horizon. Really, there was no point in having me nor anyone else in the spar. We were getting nowhere at full throttle.

An agonizing lifetime later, the Volvo slowed to idle and the *C. Michelle* ground to a halt. The small lake of water had disappeared, the pack was tightening up. The wake was gone. We were stuck.

Perry climbed up the spar and stood next to me. "You couldn't chink it any tighter with a caulking iron," he exclaimed. I agreed. "The wind is supposed to veer western, later on today," he went on to say, "It should slacken again then. Maybe I should have gone southern. It was on me mind. There's nothing we can do in this. You can go below."

That sounded good but I knew it wasn't going to be that easy. My frost-stiffened body wouldn't obey my commands and hesitantly I stooped for the ladder. Gingerly, I maneuvered from my perch and precariously turned around to begin my descent. Slowly and carefully, I made my way back down. I was thankful the boat was stopped, clutched in an icy grasp. The swells made just the slightest movement in the frosting. Out of the rigging, I beat myself with my numb limbs until the slob in my veins started to flow. Then, going below, I luxuriated in the heat, next to the hot engine, for ten minutes before I felt warm again. Time spent in the rigging was fifty-five minutes.

After wash-up with hot water, I was sipping hot tea and eating toast at my place at the table. Darrell was inside, Paul and Randy sat across, talking seals. No one was happy with the turn of events, no one was making money. "Not a one today, sir, and it's not looking good for tomorrow. There's no report of any change in the weather and we're not going anywhere until it does," Paul said emphatically, finishing the statement with a bang on the table with his knuckles. Paul wasn't pleased.

Randy shifted around a bit and twisted the lid on the jam bottle really tight, sighed and put it down. "Well boy, we're here now and there's nothing we can do about it."

Darrell made a complete shift inside me, clunking into my sore knee as he did so. "Sorry about that, my friend," he apologized, just after I sucked back my leg, grimacing.

"That's all right, Darrell, think nothing of it. From the looks of things, I'll have another day or two to get back to abnormal. Just so long as I don't come into any more hard contact with you, I think I'll be ready."

"I'll do my best," he replied, putting his hand under his jaw, sipping the last of his tea.

"The other boats are crackin' it right to 'em! I'll tell you again, it won't take long to clean up a few thousand seals. We've yet to see one!" Paul exclaimed. "Twenty-three miles is a long way ahead when we're drifting back. We're not back to where we were last night, yet!"

"That's seal hunting," Gerard said, sitting down next to me with a steaming cup of tea. I carefully shifted in closer to Darrell. "It's been no different since Abe Keans day and it'll never change," he said, clinking his spoon on the edge of his mug, looking at Paul with his eyelids shut.

No one responded to that. Paul shook his head and looked down. "We should have gone southern! The other boats went southern and they're the ones in the fat. The wind was pressing the ice on the land for a full week before we left the wharf. We'll spend our spring getting the crap beat out of us, punching ice!"

"Moose for supper, boys," David declared. "Anybody here that don't like moose with fried onions, baked potatoes and corn?"

"The only way I don't like moose is running away from me when I'm hunting 'em," Paul said in a lighter tone.

"Moose it is then."

Excusing myself from the table, I washed up the dishes that were in the sink, packed them in their places in the cupboards and went into the wheel-house. It was noon.

It wasn't too pleasant in there, either. Perry was in his chair, studying the ice report that came through on the fax. He consulted the GPS, making a few calculations, talking away to himself. Rodney was curled up in the rumble seat. He just glanced at me, then looked away. Not that it bothered me that much; we all handled the boredom and pressure in our own way.

The day had brightened a bit, the clouds retreated higher in the sky. It was a good day for killing seals. All we had to kill was time. "Three mile ahead, according to this report, there's six-tenths ice coverage," he said aloud. "That's where we need to be." Tossing the sheet of paper atop the chart table and shifting in the chair, he surveyed our dismal surroundings. According to the report, the massive ice-field had wheeled behind us, slogging Twillingate Harbor and most of the northeast coast. The southern edge of the pack was ten miles off Fogo.

There wasn't a sup of water to be seen from the wheel-house, everything was white and still. "I should have gone southern. I thought to but I figured we'd get through this way," Perry said disappointedly.

Gerard, Paul and David flooded into the wheel-house. Rodney pulled back his feet for me to pass. No one said anything. Swiveling in his chair, Perry turned up the set. Radio seals flooded the airwaves, mixed in with tales of woe, vivid descriptions of the weather and coordinates of ships "in the fat."

Gerard and Paul disappeared below when Randy and Darrell came onto the bridge. They didn't stop at all, going straight to their bunks.

A metal door opened onto the forward deck from the port side. David swung open the top half. A gust of wind ruffled papers and Rodney crunched up into a ball, as forty knots of frigid arctic winds invaded the cabin. "Close that, quick!" he exclaimed.

David pulled to the door and disappeared below. I followed him down. All the crew were awake. Climbing in atop my sleeping bag, I heard Perry grumble something about "men in bed in the middle of the day!"

"Sleep while you can aboard this one," I heard Paul mutter from below me. "Once it starts, if it starts, you might be days without closin' your eyes."

"It won't be starting today, then," Darrell remarked, "and by the looks of things, not tomorrow either. Not good!"

It wasn't good: eight men lying around in the middle of a good day while boats were rallying not far from us. As sore as I was, I wanted seals. As gory and repulsive as sealing was, I didn't want to go home with none. I had made the decision to come out here to get seals and I wanted our share but there was nothing we could do but wait. In the meantime, it was just as well to be lying in bunk as up leaning on the hard chart-table watching ice. Or in the galley looking at each other. We all wanted to be in the fat, we all handled the boredom and pressure in our own way.

The Volvo fired to life again at 4:30 P.M., followed by the first knock, ousting Gerard. Feeling pretty good and comfortable, I endured. Every time she struck, every time she veered, I thought we were gone. The sound of grating ice, of banging ice, crushing ice and exploding ice filled the forecastle to bursting. I figured any time at all a hard pan was bursting right in through beside me. Each time, the hull bounced back and finally scrunched to a dead stop. Lying on my back atop my sleeping bag, I listened. The crashing diminished to a scratching. Feeling the engine shift astern, I waited for the motion. The hull didn't withdraw immediately; the press of the floes would not let us go.

A vibration started in the stern as power increased. Gaining intensity, transforming into a shiver, it rippled through me. The shiver changed into a shudder that rattled and shook everything from the rigging to the keel. I felt the hull slowly slip astern and the sound of ice along by my ear was but a scattered thump as small fragments in the wash of the props thumped all along on both sides. Astern we slipped at full throttle, the shuddering replaced by a soothing shimmy. The main engine reduced power, the gearbox shifted ahead and the Volvo roared again. Our progress astern was halted abruptly when the aft counter brought up solid in a hard sheet. A shock wave reverberated through everything. Ahead we surged, picking up speed; the clinking sound of rubble and water, and the "whooshing" tinkle along the hull made me brace myself for the impact. Where would it be? At Darrell's ear? Maybe it would strike port side in front of David's nose.

Paul got the brunt of it, just below me. I couldn't see it but I could visualize it. The noise was deafening, the shock was bone-breaking, the lurch was violent; a seventy-degree change of course within two crunching feet at five knots. What a jolt! We didn't stop there; our momentum propelled us into another collision port side, the point of impact just abeam of where David lay. The hull rebounded to starboard, bounced off, and ground to a halt. The engine slowed, the tranny shifted into reverse, the blades chewed ice.

After twenty violent collisions, I slithered from my bunk and went up the ladder. Things out the windows looked the same to me—impregnable. We were making slow headway but the sound and feel of the ship battling invigorated me. "Come on baby, bring us to them," I said aloud, pressing myself forward against the chart table as if I might help her out in the struggle.

"Yes," Gerard said, "four hundred would be all right now. At least it would be a days pay; a big improvement over this."

The hull roused into a sheet and I was jolted to starboard. "Well, the skipper seems to be doing his best." We held on, rolling with the punches, watching the onslaught continue through the wet windows. One by one, everyone got out of bunk.

I climbed the ladder to the top deck as Perry went astern on the engine and the prop chewed ice. The bow roused into the clumper as my hands grasped the gunning table, a tremor shook through me. The forecast was partially correct; the raw, rain-infested winds had diminished imperceptibly, but the direction hadn't altered. The foreboding shroud of fog seemed to be retreating. Clouds appeared, high in the sky, and then the sun threatened to shine. The cloud cover dispersed and the sun came gleaming intensely at me from all directions. My eyes watered and my eyelids fluttered from the glare. I turned away from the brunt of it, sneezing violently four or five times.

"Bless you," I heard Perry say, "someone is wishing for you."

"I hope so, sir. Thank you. I think I need my sunglasses. I can hardly keep my eyes open."

"Protect your eyes, they are your most precious possession. I had good eyes once but I burned them up on the water. Now I got to wear these," he said, pointing to his glasses. The hull grazed a pan and we bounced sideways two or three feet.

I found that the awesome, monotonous setting often froze my stare and caused my mind to slip into its very essence, absorbing me completely. It soaked up the sounds and recorded the indifference of it all. The ice begrudgingly gave way now but that was subject to change without warning and we could expect anything out here in the floes. For now it was passively permitting us passage inch by inch.

Soon the fragrance of cooking supper floated on the bitter winds and my thoughts turned to moose. The thought didn't revolt me a bit; in fact, I looked forward to something hot and filling. I heard David say, "Tell Perry supper is ready when he is."

I relayed the message to him and he slipped the transmission in neutral. I watched Paul climb down from the rigging, his survival suit cracking with each move he made. Standing beside me, he violently shook himself warm. "After you, sir," he said, gesturing with his arm for me to pass.

"I insist," I responded, curtly stepping back a little, waiting for him to lead the way. He did without further ado.

Fifteen minutes later we were all sitting around a steaming pot at the galley table. I was squeezed between Darrell and Gerard who also shared shoulder space with David. Across from me sat Randy, crowded between Paul and Rodney, flanked by Perry, wearing his frosty, insulated coveralls. After the initial flurry of "pass me please...excuse me, boys...that looks some good..." and a blessing, we dug in like wolves. Arms passed between my nose and my plate quite frequently as we progressed into seconds.

"Did I ever tell you the story about Uncle Charlie from home?" Gerard asked, when he squeezed me together to give him room to cut the loaf of home-made bread.

"I don't think so."

"Well, Charlie reared seven children. One evening they were having supper, something like us here now, and Charlie had served up nine pork-chops. Each took one from the plate in the centre of the table, all the while eyeing the remaining one," he said, stuffing his mouth full of bread. "Did I tell you this before?"

I took a sip of tea and replied, "No, I've never heard you mention Charlie before," giving him ample time to have a few chews and a sip of tea. Everyone was waiting for the rest of it.

"As the story goes," he continued, "just at that time, the lights in the house flicked off and when they flashed back on again, there was seven forks sticking into the back of Uncle Charlie's hand."

Everyone had a great laugh at that and we chuckled down the last of supper. "That was a great scoff, Cookie," Perry said, pushing back from the table with a great gasp of air. "Now, if you'll all excuse me, I'm going to see if I can get us all in a better firing position." Standing and reaching for a toothpick, he left the galley.

"No seals today, maybe none tomorrow," Rodney casually declared, stretching his arms across the table.

Paul shifted first and responded, "We'll be lucky to see *a* seal by the look of what's out there. Other boats are cracking it to them, not a shot fired from this one, yet. I tell you, I don't like it." Darrell, shifting next to me, caused a ripple effect down through our rank, resulting in Davids getting squeezed off his end position. He stood up and disappeared through the wheel-house, leaving the dirty dishes for someone. I knew it wasn't Rodney.

No one said anything; everyone was studying something, swaying in unison, as the Volvo roared and the hull lurched ahead.

"What are you going to do, my son? "Darrell asked me. "Wash or dry?"

"I'll dry," I replied.

"Well, shift out now and let's get at it. Move, please, Gerard."

Thirty minutes later the galley was cleared away, the stove shining once more and the floor was swept and mopped clean. As I was hanging up the broom, Gerard started singing a Newfoundland ballad, in his own local twang. It sounded quite nice and I stopped to listen. On the second verse Paul joined in and added to the melody; Darrell joined in at the chorus. Randy hummed and tapped out the rhythm on the table with his hand and all together they completed the last verse rising to a crescendo, ending in a cheer and a clap from all hands. "Good job, boys," I said. "I've paid six bucks to hear worse than that."

"You haven't heard nothing yet," Gerard smiled, standing up. "But that's as much as you will hear unless you pay me three dollars."

"Sorry Gerard, I can't pay you now. By the way things are looking that might be more than I'll make this Hunt. Do you accept IOUs?"

"No problem," he replied, heading for the captain's chair.

Feeling like a chaser of cold arctic air, I went to the engine room for my heavy clothes and lined boots. As I reached for my snow-pants, the hull lurched to the starboard, hurtling me across the roaring engine. I stopped myself with my hands and upper arms pressed against the hot top-pans. My reaction was involuntary and I pushed off as the hull lurched the other way. I cracked the back of my head off the bulwark before I could catch myself. As I held on for dear life, frantically searching for footing, my hands slipped their grasp. Secure footing wasn't to be found. I fell backwards and my hip struck the wooden corner of the workbench.

I felt like screaming. The engine screamed for me; I crumpled there on the floor, flooded by pain, swearing harshly to myself. I doubted if I would last to see a seal. My arms were seared and paining, my tailbone and my hip hurt like all hell. It took some time for me to summon the energy to stand up. The pain diminished as I moved cautiously around, and cursing inwardly I climbed all the way up the ladder and limped out on deck totally convinced that I'd not survive another beating like that. I could hardly move.

I wasn't wrong to have worn my heavy clothes, but my body told me I had paid a heavy price. It had gotten noticeably colder, more biting. Our progress was minimal, to say the least. From atop the wheel-house the only water to be seen besides our pathetic wake was a tear drop in the lee of a giant iceberg, two miles to port. Other than that, it was solid white.

Perry shook his head, realizing it was a waste of time and fuel. We were going nowhere. He exited the booth and scampered up the rigging. Paul shifted over to give him room and handed him the binoculars. He scanned the horizon and shook his head. An ant atop an immense, frozen, cream pie.

Paul scurried down the ladder and shook himself in front of me. "It's not looking too good," he said. "No seals today."

I looked around and replied "I can see why."

"We'll starve to death, my son, before we see a seal," he continued, finishing his comment with his nose three inches from mine.

"I can hear you, Paul" I said, looking into his watering eyes, waiting for him to withdraw. He did and proceeded off the top deck, shaking his head as he went. Then Perry came down and stood beside me, taking off his glasses and fishing a paper towel from his pocket at the same time.

"I should have gone southern. It was in my mind, but it was such a lot further to go, I thought we might get a break."

"Break!" I exclaimed, "Break. This is a sea of breaks, a sea of heart-break."

"Yes, you're right, boy. It sure looks that way right now, don't it? I'm going down to get the forecast," he said, turning away.

I was alone on the top deck. The hull was perfectly still. The thing that struck me most was the frost: a pure, unadulterated sting of death. There was no escaping it; it made its presence known to me while I huddled in the control booth. The engine went dead and the sounds of the icepack engulfed me, freezing and solidifying around me, crunching and settling in for the night. By morning we'd be frozen in solid and nothing less than a change of wind or an "ice-breaker" would set us free. There wasn't a single seal in sight and I couldn't hear any bawling.

By eight P.M. a threatening horizon swallowed the glum evening sun and the temperature change was dramatic, ten degrees drop in ten minutes. I yearned for the heat of the cabin and a cup of hot tea. Wearily, I left the deck.

The cabin was as comfortable as I thought it would be and the tea was warming. Conversation was at a minimum. "Radio seals" were plentiful in the wheel-house, mixed in amongst the idle chatter and current emergencies: "weather conditions never as disagreeable. Ice conditions never as tough. Two men overdue in an open speedboat...hope they'll be found soon...hard night in an open boat. Over."

"Back. Yes, you're right boy. We're having a tough time of it...all day, six miles. Not worth the fuel. Dorm holed his this afternoon, backed into a pan. Pumps doing it for now, over."

"Back, yes boy, I heard him talking to CCGS *Gilbert* earlier on there...almost made a bad job of it. The *Gilbert* is assisting another boat in the Green Bay...lost a rudder. I suppose we'll get a let-up by and by. Over."

"Back. Yes, you're right, skipper, boy. Crews doing good in the southern patch off Fogo...five hundred...seven hundred today, five and six on a pan...using their speedboats....Over."

Perry sat back in his chair, taking it all in. Rodney slouched further down in the other one. "I wouldn't want to spend this night in an open boat," I said with a shiver that led me towards the forecastle ladder. "I think I hear my pillow calling me."

Rodney pulled back his legs without straightening up and stretched them out again when I passed. He said nothing so I continued my motion on towards the opening and without saying more, I disappeared from the bridge down into the tiny cabin.

Gerard's and Darrell's reading lights shone from their berths and I used their light to find mine. Switching it on, I straightened out my sleeping bag and fluffed my pillow. "Security. Security. Security," boomed in over the radio. "All stations, all stations, this is the marine weather forecast issued by Environment Canada..."

"Listen," Gerard said, even though no one was speaking...gale force warnings issued for the east coast, Funk Island Bank....Winds, northeast, forty gusting to fifty-five knots...mixed with rain and ice pellets...low tonight zero, highs tomorrow plus six."

Gerard grunted and shifted as the channel was changed or the radio was turned down. "No seals tomorrow," he said.

As I peeled my T-shirt over my sore arms, I felt no sorrow at that thought. My tailbone throbbed and my arms stung not to mention my head, my knee and my elbow. I showed my arms to Gerard before I crawled in. He drew back from them for a closer look before he asked, "How did you do that?"

After I related the incident in the engine room to him, he replied, "Yes, David did the same thing out crabbing last year. He had third-degree burns. He suffered like a dog for the whole trip. It got so bad that his arms bled through his shirt while he pulled back rope. The chafing of his rubber coat caused his arm to swell and turn blue. It was awful, he suffered like a dog."

I was taken aback by the anecdote. Really all that interested me was how to avoid the suffering. "What did he do to cure it?"

"He put some of this cream on it," he said, reaching into his stash and handing me a small bottle. "Smear some of that over your burns before you crawl in. Try to keep your arms off the covers all night."

I twisted off the top and applied a film of cream. It was cool and relieving. I rubbed it soothingly over both arms and used the excess to cool the stinging scald mark on top of both my legs. I was glad I knew Gerard. I started the manoeuvres required to get in my sleeping bag and during the shift, similar to that of sliding between two slices of bread, my tailbone and lower backbone scraped across the hard wooden frame and pain again racked my body. Finishing the gauntlet with a sideward shift, I collapsed in atop my sleeping bag with a mournful moan and a sullen sigh of relief.

"You're having a hard time getting in, aren't you boy?" he said with a grin. I turned towards him and pathetically asked, "Do you have anything for bad bruises?"

"Why?" he asked, scratching his beard to cover his grin. "How many do you have?"

"I'll put it this way," I groaned, "No less than a gallon will be any good."

"I got some A-535 that I use. It's supposed to soothe and relax sore muscles. You can have some if you want it."

We made the transfer without having to get out of bunk and I soothed my wounds with the ointment. I passed the bottle back to him and stretched out with the pungent smell of rubbing compound permeating my skin. I thought of the men out in the open boat and I found increased comfort in my bag. The room was perfectly still, murmuring voices drifted down from above and all was quiet at my ear. Beethoven slept and so did I, thirty-eight nautical miles from Twillingate, Long Point.

I woke up in a panic sometime later. It was pitch black and I didn't know where I was. My first instinctive move was to protect my face by driving my fists in the dark. They brought up solidly on the wooden bottom of Randy's bunk, six inches from my face. Yelping in pain, I frantically felt for the light switch with my numbed fingers. Randy's light came on.

"What's going on down there?" he exclaimed, coming out of his sleep. "Are you all right?"

I retreated swiftly into my cell and switched on my light. "Yes, I'm best kind, now," I lied. "I just got carried away with the thrill of it all. Thanks a lot for waking me."

"Old man, if you keeps going the way you're going, there won't be anything left of you to Hunt," I heard him say, shifting around above me, switching off his light and dropping back to sleep.

My light stayed on after that. I settled myself down and spent a lot of time studying the room. Gerard and Paul snored away. I didn't care because I knew I'd fall off at once. The comfortable sleeping bag absorbed all my sweat and fears. The thought, "What the hell am I doing here?" entered my head. "Why would any man subject himself to this misery?" I knew the answer lay within the frame of this sturdy hull.

I thought of Gerard, close to my own age. He had bills to pay and responsibilities to meet and he was part of the crew. What the ship did, he did, and over the course of it all, he earned a modest existence. "I don't mind pelting seals," he once said.

Darrell, David, and Randy were much the same. They went with the boat. Paul was slightly different. He eked out a meager living fishing with his brother and used the Hunt to get much-needed extra money. I thought of Paul at the Hunt last spring and I chuckled to myself remembering how many times I had said to him, "You're not easy, Paul." One day, last season, we had slaughtered, retrieved, butchered, washed, scrubbed, cleaned, decapitated, shifted and stowed 453 fat harps. I remembered Paul jumping for at least two hundred of them. He was not easy. This lying around, growing soft while everyone else reduced the herd, was hardest on him.

Rodney was the skipper's son. He was in a position to take over the *C. Michelle* in Perry's absence but he wasn't really sure if he wanted it or not. He did this because his father wanted him here. I figured he liked the money but he wasn't the blood and guts type man necessary to do the enormous amount of gruesome work that we hoped would have to be done. He steered the boat and did what Rodneys do.

Perry was the captain among many captains executing the Hunt. He owned the vessel. He wanted his share: a major chunk of each and every seal. Fifty per cent came off the top, first and foremost, for the boat. The sealers paid for the ammo, food, fuel, and the trucking. Perry took ten per cent. The sealers received six per cent of what was left. All clothes used in the prosecution of the Hunt had to be replaced with this money: rubber clothes, snow pants, heavy outer coat, coveralls, hooded sweaters, shirts, jogging pants, long underwear, short underwear, socks, gloves, scarf and hat because they would all end up rotten with blood, grease, sweat, and soot. You could wash them and try to keep them but within three months you'd throw them out and maybe anything packed next to them, just as in Abe Cain's time. That all totalled came to about seventeen dollars per seal for Perry and about eighty cents each for us after the seals were loaded onto a semitruck, dockside. That was based on last year's Hunt. Perry was making a few bucks, his boat was tough and, like a semi, it wasn't making any money if it wasn't moving. He always seemed to harvest enough to permit him to puff out his chest like a grouse and grin broadly while he entertained friends, family and fellow captains that always visited during the off-loading or while we were cleaning the boat from stem to stern, inside and out, top and bottom after discharging was finished.

Me...I figured I was in a boat most similar to Paul's. I'd struggled for twelve years to maintain a steady job unsuccessfully. I endured this misery for the money. It was one of the ways that enabled me to keep my income in the "barely respectable" bracket. Other than that, my future depended on how much the Japanese were willing to pay my boss to load their capelin or crab on their ship. My job was to operate a forklift and if last season was an indicator, I figured my miles on the lift this season would be a lot less, if any at all.

Prior to that, I had charged my fisheries boss with three violations under the fisheries act and that hadn't turned out too well for me. I was a sworn warden at the time, with five years experience. That didn't seem to account for much because the following year I didn't get the position back. "Federal government cutbacks," they told me. To add insult to injury, my fisheries boss never appeared in court to face the charges; instead he was given a promotion. I fought them tooth and nail for a long time, but, finding little support, I drew back for fear of losing what I had. I found out later, while searching for other work, that they had attacked my reputation, making it hard for me to find any. I found work here.

Crack! The sound shot through the forecastle bringing everyone out of his sleep. "What was that, boys, a gunshot?" I heard Gerard shout as I came awake. A couple reading lamps came on, making up a total of three. I saw Gerard hanging half out of his bunk. David had his head poked out looking down at Gerard.

"Pressure coming on the ice," Gerard said with a yawn. "Boys, we're under pressure." As he finished talking the hull made a perceptible tilt to starboard, then the light came on in the wheelhouse. We all waited anxiously in our tombs for the word.

The reflected glare from the spotlight lit up the tiny space as Perry turned the beam about. "I can't see anything out of the ordinary. Ice settling, I suppose," I heard him say, as he turned the light about. "I can't see very far with the snow. It must be thirty-five westerly out there now. I wonder if they found those men in that speedboat?"

"Never heard any word," I heard Rodney respond.

"Forget seals today," I heard Randy say, shifting and switching off his light. "No seals today."

"The quota will be over and forgot about and we won't see a one," Paul said. His light went out. "Not a single one."

I switched off my light; there was plenty flooding in from above. Settling back, I became aware of the howl of the wind outside. I heard the "ticks" of the ice crystals striking the fiberglass hull beside me and I tried to envision being out in an open boat. I wasn't in "God's pocket," but, for now, I was warm and comfortable. I took comfort from that and realized that an hour in the rigging was a picnic.

Wednesday, April 9

The skipper had us all up at 7:00 A.M. sitting and standing around. We were dressed in outside wear and we were all studying a rent in the crust, about two hundred yards off our starboard. The vein of ink-blue water stretched northeast to southwest for about two miles. In the raw westerly wind, that was the limit of our view. Everything else was a monotonous, menacing soup of white and grey. The smell of bacon and eggs waffled on the wind and David sounded the breakfast call.

We all ate together and after the blessing, Perry paused in his eating to say, "I don't know how to read that rent. It might be a good sign, the pressure is easing and we might use it as a way out. It might be the weak strand of the web, the place that's destroyed first when the pressure increases. Right now, I can't tell."

Gerard reached across me for the jam, "We'll pray for the best and prepare for the worst, then we'll wait and see."

Perry was first to finish. He left the galley and we heard the main engine start. We felt the transmission shift but we remained still. By the time I had finished my tea the Volvo had shut down again. "We're stuck fast like fresh crap to a wool blanket," Paul said, reaching for the jam jar.

"None of that language at the table!" Gerard scolded him. But it was too late; he had it said. I wondered silently where the CCGS *Gilbert* was working.

"Let's prepare to abandon ship, gentlemen," Paul said, making a gesture for Randy and Rodney to let him out. "What are you taking, Darrell?"

My first thought was for warm spare clothes, but then I thought, "Who am I kidding? Where am I going to run?" If this ice-field broke up, shattered with us in it, the only chance we had was with the ship. I visualized us on the tilted back deck, chopping frantically at the ever-encroaching floes with axes. "I think I'll get dressed," I said.

Just in case, we prepared the speedboat for launching, and loaded gas and water. The food bag wasn't yet filled. We waited and watched.

At 9:00 A.M., I was getting stir crazy. Grabbing a gaff, I jumped over the rail onto the frozen ocean. The crust crunched beneath my boots. Casually I ventured forth in search of my "ice-legs." Fifty yards from the boat, I heard someone say, "Where are ya goin'?" Looking back, I saw Randy standing on the deck.

"Didn't I tell you, I quit. I'm going home. See you later."

"You're going the wrong way," he called back. "Home is that way." Using his arm, he pointed in a direction on the opposite side of the long-liner.

"Oh. Then I'll just go for a walk, stretch my legs, take in some of the scenery, hopefully meet a few of the neighbours, maybe go see a movie, you know?"

"Wait for me. I'll join you if you don't mind."

"I don't mind at all." I milled around and waited. The ship was riding high on the floes, like a beached blue whale. Randy appeared, grabbed a gaff, jumped over the rail and walked toward me.

"Let's go look at the rent," he said.

As he passed in front of me, I felt the crust rumble beneath my feet, before the report of the noise arrived. *Crack*! The tremor shook Randy to the topping. My gaff kept me up.

Randy scurried to his feet but the noise was gone before he was all the way up. "Another rent," he said, shaken. "Let's go back and have another look." I followed him back aboard.

Atop the bridge, the crew was turned away from us, pointing off the port bow. By the time we got there it was no trouble to see the fresh wound. It was a mere two hundred yards from the bow, running basically parallel to the other one, outside of us. We were smack in the middle.

During lunch, we felt another tremor shake the hull. Reconnaissance from the spar revealed no visible fracture. Perry tried the main engine again. It was useless.

After lunch, I felt jumpy, wanting to finish my walk. "I'm finishing my stroll in a few minutes, Randy. Are you coming with me?

"Yes, I'm right behind you." I reached for a gaff and jumped from the rail. Randy jumped out behind me.

"Don't forget to write," Darrell laughed, as we struck out for the water vein. Nothing moved; everything was frozen solid. We passed our shakedown point of the morning and continued on a haphazard course to the closest inky blue water. Some of the ice clumpers stood taller than me and in the glow of the faint sun, they seemed indifferent and obliging.

It felt good to be away from the confines of the boat. To be able to make fifty steps without turning or climbing a ladder gave me a great sense of freedom and I stretched out my stride, hopping atop the high clumpers and weaving between those too tall to climb. Then we reached the rent.

It stretched in a relatively straight line, extending as far as we could see from atop a tall clumper of ice, at least two miles long and forty yards wide— a perfect channel for the *C. Michelle*. The thirty-five-knot westerly winds created a slight ripple on the surface. We were lounging in the lee of the biting winds when I saw a seal break the surface. Randy saw him just as he reared his head and looked at us. It was an old dog harp. He dived again and Randy said excitedly, "I'm going for the gun!"

Before I could reply, he was gone. I watched the water and saw the seal appear again, playing behind a knob of ice, leisurely bobbing in the icy water, oblivious to the cold and to me. He was gone again by the time Randy scampered up beside me with his .243 Remmington. "I'll see, now, if this one is on or not," he said, taking off his gloves and loading four cartridges into the magazine. I scanned the pool in hopes of seeing the fish-eater again.

"Yes, put the bullet in him first chance you get," I said, shifting around, stretching my neck for a better view. Randy pushed the bolt to with a distinct "click." I experienced an adrenaline rush. Scanning the pool, I said, "Now, Mister Harp, show yourself."

He appeared again, sixty yards away, up and across the blue ripples. Randy shifted the rifle and took aim through the scope. As the old dog reared in a "peek-a-boo" way to take a look at us, the rifle fired and I heard the thud of bullet meeting bone. A puff of fur shot into the air on impact and the seal rolled quietly over in the water. The smell of burnt gunpowder whisked on the wind blasting up my nostrils. "Good shot, Randy. You got 'em!"

Randy stood up, ejected the shell, laid the rifle, in "bolt-open" position, beside him, and said, "That rifle is deadly and he's not the only one around."

"Right on! There's thirteen million of them frequenting these floes and we got one. First blood! Now, how do we get him?"

Strangely, the dead seal appeared to be floating closer to us, contrary to the wind. We rationalized that the tide exerted an effect far greater than that of the wind. It quietly bled out about two gaff-lengths from us when we felt the rumble and discerned a distant roar. Large vibration-waves ripped the surface of the lead. Looking in the direction of the increasing roar, I saw chaos advancing down the crack.

Somewhere to the north, tide and wind pressed in on the ice-mass; maybe it had come in contact with the land. In any case, it crashed the lead closed, forcing ice upwards and downwards, advancing faster than a man could run. "Run!" I shouted, pushing off from my perch and heading for the boat.

Randy grabbed up his rifle in mid-stride and vaulted across the sheet in an attempt to keep up with me. The roar intensified as we zigzagged around and between the pinnacles. As the water in the rent closest to us slammed shut like a trap, the ice under my feet shook violently and the tremor shook us both down. Crouching low, hanging onto my gaff, I watched as the pressure ridge "freight-trained" south, passing us by and taking the violence along with it.

The sound and sight of pans foundering in on each other jolted me back to reality and we both stood up.

"Quick boys, come aboard!" Turning, I saw the crew hastily waving to us. We went without delay, much relieved to climb over the rails.

The crew's attention was focused on the pressure ridge. They hardly noticed as we made our way up behind them. When I saw the scene, it stopped me in my tracks. The other rent was closing up. We bore silent witness to its awesome power as it explosively drove the colliding edges skyward successively down the fracture. The tremendous noise resounded into the ice-field leaving behind in its wake the sounds of ice crashing down on itself. Thundering off, we were left dumbfounded, humble, and helpless.

Then the hull listed slightly to starboard. Everyone noticed the tilt and we all looked at each other.

"The pressure's on," Gerard said, smashing the silence the floes held on us. "That's not good."

Nobody responded to that; we just milled around the top deck, unconsciously making a visual check of the speedboat, each thinking his own thoughts. "Beam me up, Scottie!"

We all knew what we could expect. As the pressure increased, our chances of escaping unscratched diminished. Being flanked by twenty-foot pressure ridges was not good. I remembered back to my first Hunt in the Gulf.

Pressure ridges were common there that spring. I had gotten used to climbing and dragging pelts over them. Two other sealers and myself were working, panning seals about a mile from the ship. We had a flag flying above one hundred pelted whitecoats when we heard it coming. Taking nothing but our knives we scurried for the boat. The pressure passed us with a body-seizing roar. On both sides of us, the crust exploded, behind us and in front of us. There was nowhere left to run. Paralyzed, we huddled together, watching nature run its rampageous course. It was three or four terrifying minutes before the noise faded, leaving only the chilling sound of grinding, foundering ice. We climbed over three ice-ridges in an attempt to find our seals. We spotted a piece of the blood pan but found no trace of our pelts, our gaffs or our lunch-bags. The ice-field had shattered into pieces, each sheet surrounded by a wall of ice.

And so, on the *C. Michelle*, we passed the long, uneasy hours of a good day for killing seals. There were no seals around us, nothing but frozen sea for as far as the eye could see. Mile after nautical mile of white. We hung around the deck, we climbed atop the bridge, and we even climbed the spar. We'd meet in the galley, we'd pass in the hall. We'd put on the kettle and take off the kettle, we'd dirty the dishes and clean the dishes, and we'd look through books we were tired of looking through. Then we'd brush past one another in the hall again, all in thirty minutes. No one talked much; it was all said. We were all aware of "no change." Then we all felt a slight vibration and discerned an encroaching, muffled noise. The hair on the back of my neck tingled. Perry was the first to run for the deck. We scurried out behind him.

Off to the eastern horizon the noise erupted, rising to a crescendo as it advanced. The ice gripping the hull began to scrunch its way up another few inches, listing us further. Shifting for balance we all heard the sound of glass breaking in the galley. No one paid it any heed. Huddled together, we helplessly watched the pressure ridge come, splitting the crust asunder. As if in slow motion, the first swell rolled beneath us, causing the sheet to shatter. The next swell lifted us higher, pressing the jagged pieces together like the grating of teeth. Sinking into the trough, the ice stretched apart as if to swallow, then rose again as if to chew it.

We watched, spellbound, as the pressure ridge came alive and started eating itself. Grinding ice sheets, three feet thick, were squeezed out of the water up into the frosty air. Crashing down from atop the peak, the large pans blended in perfectly with the clouds frozen to the white horizon. They crashed down atop the floes, bleeding blue water, smashing and tumbling and exploding all to the roar of a thousand freight trains.

Eighty yards from disaster, Perry started the main engine. It roared to life in a cloud of black smoke. We stood around him, cocked to spring into action no matter what that might entail. In the meantime, we watched in fascination as an ice-field was smashed to bits all around us. In the churn and mix of it all, we began to move as Perry poured on the power. He turned the bow to face the oncoming swells and the hull scrunched free.

The swell increased to two metres; the sheet diminished to mulch. The pressure eased as the troughs spread it abroad. *Bang*! A wheeling sheet whopped the bow and we all lurched to port. Perry hastily regained control and headed us into the ice-waves. The fractured pressure ridge, a twenty-foot wall of tangled ice sheets, bobbed and swayed and blocked our way.

"That's the way out," Perry said to no one in particular, turning the bow to confront the barrier. Nobody spoke as he leaned forward, setting tight his lower jaw.

As we fought our way toward the ice-sentinels, the long-liner was holding her own. The engine roared and the hull shivered and shook, the props chewed into the submerged sheet, the wake foamed and hissed as wet spinning chunks of ice seethed to the surface. Perry never slackened the throttle.

The wall split asunder in the movement of the increasing sea, blasted into smaller and smaller fragments. Swallowed by the increasing swells, they rolled and swayed and crashed into the water. We rolled and rocked, twisted and turned, banged and punched, reeled and fought our way forward. We were all very much relieved and very happy to be moving under our own power even if the going was treacherous and slow. The powerful swells from a distant storm were crashing their way to the northeast and to the patch of seals we had heard so much about and wanted to meet so badly. Cautiously, we weaved in their wake.

The galley was a state: paper plates, mugs, bottles and shards of glass strewn across the seats, table and floor. We all pitched in and cleaned it up, mopping the floors in the companionway, head, skipper's room and wheelhouse while we were at it. Conversation was at a minimum but we were all happy to be able to do it.

At 6:00 P.M. we saw our first young harp. It was a fat whitecoat, crying alone on a rocking pan. Its mother bobbed in the slob close by, nervously watching her pup. As we crashed closer, he reared his head and screeched at us. He was fat and prime, weighing around seventy-five pounds. To say a baby harp seal's coat is white is not accurate; it's as yellow as much as it is white. Their faces are cute, there's no doubt about that; big, black, watering eyes. Big enough to enable me to see my reflection each and every time I viciously bashed in their skulls with my gaff.

Yellowish-white fur covers a harp seal's face. Above the eyes two black spots indicate eyelashes. The body bulges out big around the shoulders, and there are soft wrinkles in the fur of his flippers. The body torpedoes out down the back, ending in two fur-covered rear-scutters. This seal's opened mouth revealed sharp teeth that I knew would give anyone a bad bite. Crashing closer, he clawed his way across the pan with his scratchers, his plump body moving with a fat-rolling gait away from us, screeching continuously in short, "cat-like" bawls that got on my nerves before we were abreast of the beast. At the crushed fringe, where his mother bobbed, it stopped and bawled pathetically to her. Her large black head moved back and forth, her concerned eyes nervously shifting from the wailing pup to us.

"Someone take a gaff and shut that up," Paul said, kicking the gunnel with his boot.

The seal had nothing to fear from us; we were not allowed to harvest whitecoats. In a week's time, the fat little fish-eater would shed his white fur for a coat of grey and he'd be fair game. How stupid that is! I guess it looks nicer to the general public, but to us in the floes hunting seals, it didn't make much sense. A bullet in the brain now, or in a few days' time: what was the difference? We are only allowed to kill so many so what difference does colour make? None.

"He's not started to turn, yet," Perry stated as we ricocheted past. "I figured they'd be all turned by now."

"Must be a late bloomer," Gerard said, peering down at the bawling baby.

"Goodness, I hope they're not all like that!"

That was not a good sign. The money was in prime beaters, whitecoats after they molt their fur. The molting phase takes about a week to complete and during that time the pelts are worth less than half of prime. We watched and listened to it fall away astern. Fifty yards away, the old bitch surged upon the pan with remarkable speed. Only the dark gray of her fat belly touched the sheet; her head was held high on a stretched neck, her lower back and rear scutters arched toward the clouds. Her powerful front flippers supported her four hundred pounds. Bawling continuously, the pup crawled up beside her. A small speck of life pulsing on a bleak ocean of certain death. I turned my attention back to the bow.

It reminded me again of my time at the Hunt in the Gulf when we had lived for three days amid a herd of two million harps. We had made surprisingly good time and we were tucked in the herd, waiting for the Hunt to begin. The whitecoats bawled all morning, they bawled all evening, they bawled each night and they grew bigger and bigger. The only time they stopped bawling was during feeding time when the mothers nursed them. During those times, I'd climb into the barrel in the spar and scan the floes. The huge mothers dotted the ice-field like specks of pepper on a gigantic white sheet. I have never seen as many animals in one place since. I had my doubts if I would see it this year.

"Another one there," Paul said from the spar, and I looked to see him pointing off the starboard bow.

I heard the screeching before I saw the fur. The mother bobbed in the water next to it, looking anxiously at us. The pup spotted her and lumbered in its rolling gait to the edge of the pan. She rose from the water in reassurance before slipping back beneath. As we crashed past at a steady three knots, the pup turned its attention to us, bawling and cocking its head in a threatening gesture, baring its teeth and screeching.

"You're a sassy little one, aren't you?" I heard Darrell say to the bawling fish-eater, "Boys, that's two in a row. Not good."

Perry went below and returned with my .222 rifle, and six boxes of ammo. Rodney took over the controls while we tied a piece of thick foam to a life-jacket and he and Gerard secured it to the top of the gunning table built at the extreme forward edge of the wheel-house. He filled the magazine of the rifle before placing it atop the cushion in "bolt-open" position. That done, he puffed out his chest, and placed the field glasses to his eyes, saying, "Come on now."

It was frosty and raw on the top deck but the sight of the rifle quelled the shivers and I felt a surge of adrenaline. There was still plenty of time for a hundred before dark but Paul was quiet in the rigging, the gun silent in its case.

Then the knives came out. The sounds of steel on stone, steel on steel mingled with the sounds of crunching ice. A razor-sharp knife was a necessity; anything less was no good. Mine was a wooden-handled "Red River" type with a curved, eight-inch blade. I carefully rubbed it with the stone reflecting back to my first sealing knife and putting the edge on that.

It had been during that same trip to the Gulf. I was sixteen at the time and I asked an old sealer if he would sharpen my new knife for me. There was a large, round sharpening stone aboard and the man replied, "Yes, if you spin the stone." I agreed and half an hour later I was getting tired, after changing hands a couple of times. The old sealer ignored me, guiding the blade across the wetted stone, turning it now and again so as to sharpen both sides evenly.

After an hour my arms were falling off and my neck hurt like hell but I didn't want to say anything to the old sealer. Finally, the second hour passed and not able to stand any more, I said, "That's good enough," and stopped spinning the wheel.

The look he gave me startled me. "You asked me to sharpen your knife, didn't ya?" he asked.

Frightened half to death, I stammered out, "Yes, sir, I did."

"You said you would spin the wheel?"

"Yes, sir."

"Then spin it!"

"Yes sir!" I responded promptly, grabbing the handle and spinning the wheel for all I was worth. He didn't find the edge he sought until long after the crew had gone for dinner. But what an edge it was! Any time, that entire spring, when the edge dulled from cutting fur and bones, I had only to rub it a few times with my new steel and it was back to razor-sharp again.

"Sharpen mine for me when you get yours done, will you?" Darrell asked, coming up beside me with a brand-new knife.

"Yes, no problem," I replied with a chuckle.

We followed in the wake of the swells parading to the northeast, making very good progress. We were still getting beaten around a lot. As I was putting the final touches on my knife, one violent collision sent a shock wave through me which caused me to slice open the thumb of my left hand. Blood dropped on the deck. Turning to Darrell who was watching me, I said, "Wouldn't you know. The first blood on her deck this spring is mine."

"That's a deep cut you got there. You got to be careful, now, that you don't get sealer's finger."

That was all I needed, blood poisoning. Inspecting my wound, I saw that it was cut deep enough for one stitch. "I got to go in and take care of it."

The miles dwindled on the GPS, and the herd eluded us. It was a big ocean, and there was lots of room to hide. We all looked for the telltale blackspot atop the gleam of white. I found it perishing to stand around, looking for leads, looking for seals, looking at ice rising and ice falling, ice in front, ice behind, ice to both sides, ice, ice, ice as far as I could squint. The only break in the barren white was the foaming green of the short "snake" trailing astern. Even the gulls had quit following us. The floes seemed to be going together; the smashed fragments were getting bigger, their ominous weight ironing out the wrinkles made by the ocean swells. The ice seemed to become more reluctant, harder to get along with. A continuous plume of black smoke from the stacks and an adamant growl from the Volvo produced slow passage. Weaving our way left and right, we advanced towards the encroaching arctic night. Dusk found us locked in tight, frigid temperatures with not one seal on deck, not one in sight and not a single seal of the immense harp herd to be heard.

The Volvo shut down at 9 P.M. All was crispy-quiet on the eastern front. The squalling wind was high, morale was low. "Radio-seals" by the thousands shot through the bridge while we eavesdropped on the news of the day. Perry was in his chair, his head held in his hands. He listened quietly, sometimes shifting around. I stood beside the port side metal door. A sheen of frost crusted it, drops of water dripped onto the floor. Rodney slouched in the rumble seat, his hand under his jaw, not inclined for conversation. Careful not to step in the pool of water, I listened along with them.

The men lost in the open boat were found shortly before 10 P.M. none the worse for their experience. One vessel reported a hole in its hull and rudder damage. The crew were holding their own with the help of pumps. Another reported it was sinking, the crew preparing to abandon ship. *CCGS Gilbert* was enroute to assist. Another captain mentioned that the seals were numerous where he was located, adding that his tally for the day was seven hundred. All the boats had picked up a lot of prime beaters. Perry listened to it all from his chair, having none to add himself. I went below.

The crew was settled in; all but Darrell's berth burned a light. Randy and David wore earphones attached to their walkmans. I slipped out of my clothes and, without incident, climbed in the bag, pulling it up over my shoulders. It felt really good and I reflected back to the many times today that I had yearned for this moment.

"All stations. All stations. All stations. This is the marine weather forecast issued by Environment Canada...." a tinny voice said over the radio on the bridge.

"Listen," Gerard said, even though no one was talking. Uninterrupted, the voice finished its report.

"We might get a few tomorrow, by the looks of things," Paul said. "Four hundred would be a good start. Worst part of it is, we don't make a cent from the first five hundred. I think that's a shocking high price to pay for maybe a one-way ticket out here."

A solid floe soundly struck the hull as he finished talking, sending a nudge reaction through me as the words sank in. "Go ahead, Paul. Make my day," I responded, turning on my back, gently placing my sore arm over my eyes, thinking of all the work, the gore, the petrifying cold, and the dangers involved in the first five hundred.

"Put some more cream on your burns before you go to sleep," Gerard said, digging the bottle from his stash and passing it to me. As I reached over to get it from him, a drop of water struck my arm. "Sweat from the skylight," he said. It was after the lights were all turned out and I was searching for some light that I noticed that the styrofoam covering the skylight was removed and an ample supply of light filtered in through the glass, looking soft and reassuring. No claustrophobia attacks tonight.

"Thanks boys," I said to no one in particular as I shifted to find that extra-comfortable spot. No one responded. The tiny cabin was filled with the sounds of the Hunt; ice nibbled, the gusting wind snicked snow crystals off the hull inches from my ear, settling sheets nudged us, men snored, the cradle was all but still. Beethoven rested and so did we, in a quiet harbor, amid heavy-ice coverage, forty-five nautical miles from ice-clogged Long Point.

THURSDAY, APRIL 10

The sound of the generator around 5:30 A.M. heralded the start of a new day. In the comfort of the sleeping bag, I wondered if any harps could hear us. Soon the wraps of comfort would have to be shed and the ultimate misery would begin. I didn't mind it so much once the fray started; it was the prelude that was hardest. I knew this crew could handle four hundred per day. It would be extremely taxing and agony-intensive the first three days as we worked off the layers of leisure and plenty from our bodies. Muscles sprained; ligaments torn; hands slashed, bleeding and sore. Backs breaking, legs cramping, shoulders aching, stomach retching and it all started with the report of the rifle.

Bang! The cabin lurched and the hull shook as the long-liner surged forward with a sense of renewed vigour. Gerard hopped out, quickly dressed and scrambled up the ladder. I knew it was just a matter of time for me so I resigned myself sleepily to follow his lead.

Golden rays of sunshine illuminated the bridge, instantly lifting my spirits. The windows were dry and visibility was excellent. Slipping into the rumble seat, I sat back to witness the beauty of the morning.

Gerard was in the captain's chair, studying the dials and pushing a few buttons. Perry was in the booth atop the roof. "This is going to be a nice day. We should get a few today. They'll be crawling up somewhere when it warms up."

"Yes sir," I replied. "I hope we're right in the middle of them."

It was far from warm outside. It reminded me of mornings in January, ice fishing. The tide of the southbound Labrador Current loosened the floes, swatches of gun-metal blue water reflected the early morning sun. By the looks of it, it was going to be the best kind of a day. Later on, if the floes kept going abroad, if we got into the seals, conditions would be ideal for using the speedboat: glassy-smooth water infested with large sheets of seal-bearing ice.

These floes were higher, the drifting snows filled in all the hollows, the wind smoothed off the edges. The sea eroded into "cauliflower, top-heavy," multi-layered pans. Frozen snow formed overhangs giving the "jumper" a false sense of security. In the glow of the morning sunrise they looked soft and friendly.

"If you got sunglasses, wear them today," Gerard said. "That sun will blind you when it gets some power."

"Yes sir." I didn't need snow-blindness. I had witnessed a man lying three days in bunk suffering like a whipped dog from it. He said it was like having his eyeballs sanded. They watered and burned continuously.

The hull collided with a sheet and we braced ourselves against the shock. "The skipper is driving her this morning," Gerard said, "He can almost smell them up there, now."

"Well, that's what we're here for, the bloody things. Come on with three thousand!"

The noise and shock drove Paul from his berth. "It's a great morning, isn't it?"

"Yes, it's beautiful."

I was a beautiful day for hunting and we knew that at any time we could expect a shot. We were ready, eager and willing to start and we scrutinized the floes as we scrunched past.

At 1:00 P.M., Paul spotted our first "beater," alone on a large pan, three hundred yards ahead. At seventy-five yards it detected us and lifted its head to look in our direction. Perry loaded the rifle and at fifty yards, Rodney cut the engine. It was not an easy target to hit. We rocked in the barely noticeable swells and the seal shifted on the pan. The intent is to put the bullet in the brain, not only to deliver instantaneous death but also to ensure a number-one pelt. If the bullet enters or exits anywhere behind the front flippers, the pelt is number-two, worth twelve dollars instead of twenty-six.

Bang! The crisp arctic air was split asunder by the report of the rifle. The harp's head dropped to the pan and stayed absolutely still. The Hunt was on.

"Good shot, skipper," Paul shouted from the spar. I smelled the burnt gunpowder.

Rodney opened the throttle, black smoke belched from the stack and the boat charged forward to claim the prize. We made for the aft deck to retrieve it.

"Jumping," any sealer will tell you, is the hardest and most dangerous job of all, due to the simple fact that one must leave the boat, make his way across the undulating floes, claim the seal with a gaff and return safely to the deck. I was eager to go, eager for a run to warm myself up. Selecting a gaff from the rack, I said, "He's my puppy, now." With one leg hung out over the starboard gunnel, I waited for him to come into view.

Ice crunched along the hull as the blood-pan came closer and I waited for my time to pick a spot on the slippery pan to land. Springing from the gunnel, I was going through the air when the hull struck the floe with a loud *Crunch!*, sending cold shivers up my crystal spine.

The snowy surface was hard and slippery after the night's cold and my boots hardly penetrated the crust. The seal lay twenty yards across the sheet and, running up to it, I stuck the hook of my gaff into the blood-spurting bullet hole in its skull. Turning back to the boat, I dragged it behind me. Conditions were ideal for retrieving and in no time I was back to the boat. Rodney kept the hull pressed to the pan, Perry watched from the top deck, the crew waited on the stern. Stopping next to the hull, I passed the handle of the gaff to Gerard. Bending down, I grabbed the seal by the hind scutters, lifted it upwards, throwing it inwards the same time he pulled. The young harp thudded onto the deck. Carefully watching my footing I reached for the rope hanging over the side to which a car tire was tied. Timing it exactly right, I jumped for the tire and reached for the rope. The Volvo roared and the smoke belched. I pulled myself in over the rail as we charged towards the next target. Taking a deep breath of frosty, clean air, I watched the blood-pan fall away astern, a thin thread of crimson red, on a pan of glistening white, ending abruptly in the green of the sea. Number one was aboard. "If only they were all that easy," I thought.

"My misery starts here," said Darrell, rubbing the brand-new blade of his knife on a steel. "Here begins the bloody mess." Tossing the steel on the hatch-cover, he positioned the dead harp, belly up between his feet, bent over and placed the blade against the seal's bottom lip saying, "You bloody thing!"

The sculping of a seal takes an experienced sealer about two minutes. It involves nearly one hundred precise cuts, slashes, gashes, slits, slices, splits, and hacks. It involves bending over and straightening up six times. It involves three shifts around the profusely bleeding body. It involves placing one's face into the cloud of pungent, warm steam that rises from the blood-dripping conglomerate of entrails that in dog hoods could weigh sixty repulsive pounds. It involves grabbing the black, warm, twitching carcass, lifting it and tossing it down in the swath. It is, in every sense of the word, bloody, backbreaking, repulsive, revolting, gory work in the "beast" of times. Add to that the bitter cold: howling, merciless winds flecked with ice and snow, on a deck underfoot that gets more slippery than two eels making babies in a barrel of mucus. Add to that the sudden lurching of the hull, the razor-sharp knives and very close quarters, spread evenly over hour after horrific hour from long before dawn until way past dusk, day after day after day—if we are lucky.

I watched Darrell bend over and with one continuous, smooth, cut, slit the seal open from the bottom of the lip, through the centre breast, severing the penis and the navel, stopping at the tail. The chest split apart to a depth of two inches, exposing the thick, oily, breast-white fat and the dark rib cage. Blood sloshed out around his boots and pungent steam enveloped his head as the next slash opened the rib cage, exposing the vital organs.

Cutting the windpipe and grabbing it with his gloved left hand, he pulled and cut his way down the carcass, finishing with a few careful cuts around the anus. Straightening up, he held the steaming, blood-dripping conglomerate of organs in his hand. Turning, he tossed it over the rail. Ice gulls fought for it in the wake.

Bending again, he positioned the blade at the right side of the seal's jaw and with a smooth, steady stroke, started to remove the pelt, which fell away from the body and lay flat on the deck as he continued to cut deeper in towards the backbone. The fore shoulder (flipper) stayed with the pelt. Shifting the blade to the opposite jaw, he repeated the process down the other side. When the pelt lay flat on deck, he shifted, slipping in the oozing blood and grease, to position himself over the carcass. Bending, he punctured the soft bones of the rib cage with his knife. Plunging his fingers in the wound, he lifted the body off the pelt, carefully cutting the pelt from the backbone. This upward pull (of about fifty pounds) often lifts the pelt off the deck. At times when the deck is awash with blood and gore, this action causes a distinct, repulsive slurping sound. With the pelt separated from the backbone, he released his grip, letting the steaming body flop back onto the fat. Shifting back a little, Darrell continued by grabbing the right rear flipper. With the knife, he cut carefully around the soft bone, separating the fur and severing the tailbone with a slash. Changing his grip to the other flipper he cut the fur from the bone and the pelt fell away. He then tossed the body back over its head. The steaming, thirty pound chunk of dark meat landed with a spattering of blood.

Bending again, he located the shoulder with his blood-dripping hand and, grabbing it, he pulled upwards, making a slash parallel to the deck. Lifting and cutting with quick, decisive movements, he cut the pelt away, peeling the shoulder down towards the wrist, forming a "sock" of fur. As the scratchers came into view, he cut the shoulder free of the pelt with a swipe. Straightening up again, he tossed the steaming flipper into the empty tub. Wiping his nose with the bloody glove, he slip-slid around to the opposite end where the head remained attached.

Bending again, he grabbed the steaming corpse by the neck, lifting it upwards. Since seals are shot through the brain this area was usually the messiest. Severe swelling caused massive blood clots that exploded and rushed over his hand. He focused his blade in the area where the skin hung from the shattered skull. Pieces of bone and brain mixed with the steaming blood to form an ooze of gore that made the shifting deck treacherous. Fighting for stability, he cut the fur from the skull bone; the eyes burst and flowed and mixed with the swath as he proceeded down the bridge of the seals nose, to the whiskers. The pelt was now free of the body. Picking up the steaming, gruesome, twitching carcass, he tossed it towards an axe stuck in a wooden block. It landed with a squish and a spray of blood that spattered the gunnel. He didn't care. He bent again and felt for the remaining shoulder and, locating it, lifted it upwards before employing his blade to repeat the flipper-removing process.

That done, he bent again and grabbed the pelt through the eye holes and, slipping all the way, he dragged it back on the stern for washing.

Gerard decapitated the carcass with the axe and severed the two hind flippers. He tossed it into the stern corner and threw the head and flippers overboard. "You'll eat no more of our fish!" he said. "Turn on the water."

I turned on the hydraulic pump and slobby seawater blasted from the hose. Darrell sprayed off the deck before blasting the blood from the fat. He turned it over and blasted the blood from the fur while Gerard scrubbed it with a long-handled brush. Satisfied that it was clean enough, he slid the pelt to the stern, stowing it "fat-down." Number one was secured. Spraying down the gunnels and spraying off his rubber clothes, he shouted, "Come on with another three thousand of the bloody things!"

That's the way the day went. It was a great day for hunting seals but there were few to hunt. We didn't get enough to keep me warm. Once, while we huddled in the lee, Darrell asked, "Can you remember the first time you jumped for a seal?"

I told him and Gerard about my first Hunt in the Gulf of St. Lawrence, off the Magdalene Islands, aboard the *Gulf Star*, with my father, the captain. It was before the Hunt started and I was in the wheel-house dressed in shirt and slippers with eight other sealers. We were butting through heavy ice when a whitecoat passed too close to the rail for my father to resist. Stopping the ship, he looked at me and said, "Over the side, Mickey. Get that seal." Obeying orders, I ran out on deck, grabbed my bat and tow-rope, climbed down the side-sticks, ran up to the bawling whitecoat and cracked it on the skull three times. Hooking my tow-hook into its mouth, I ran back to the ship, tossed the line up to someone on deck before climbing back aboard to see the dead whitecoat and the fisheries officer looking at me.

"Did you kill that seal?" he asked.

"Yes, sir."

"Who told you to kill it?"

"The captain, sir."

The officer told me that I could lose my license. No one was permitted aboard without a license so I would be charged and flown to the Magdalene Islands by chopper and I'd have to find my own way home, at my expense. This was devastating news for me and I stood there shocked and guilty. He left to see my father. They spent the next twenty minutes in the captain's room in conference. No charges were laid.

Darrell and Gerard seemed to enjoy my account. We felt the hull stop, followed by the report of the gun. *Bang! Bang!* "Over the side, Mickey," Gerard said. I grinned and picked out a gaff.

I didn't mind jumping. I didn't mind running and vaulting across the moving, shifting pans, dragging back seals that were sometimes three times heavier than me. I dreaded landing on the ice and jumping for the tire. I didn't mind the gore or the hours, but, barring seasickness, I hated nothing more than being huddled next to the hot hydraulic lines, clinging to warmth with my skeleton rattling inside my clothing. That was misery for me. On the floes, I was alive, my heart pumped faster, butterflies filled my stomach, and sometimes, my head steamed and sweat ran down my body from the exertion. In the idle times, it froze on my skin. My body temperature soared and plummeted from one extreme to the other, time and time and time again.

At 8:30 P.M. Perry shut down for the night, and we had thirty seals stowed. Not a lot of money. None were in very good spirits when we washed each other down with the frigid water blasting from the hose. Floodlights in the spar illuminated the frosty scene. My turn came and I stepped out front. "Put up your hood," Darrell said, holding the brush. His eyes glowed white from a mask of brown, his own oilskins shining with grease and smeared with blood. Then the water struck my back.

The little heat I had remaining in my body was whooshed away and in its draft swooped in the cold. I shivered and gritted my teeth while Gerard blasted me and Darrell scrubbed me. "Lift your arms," he said, and as I did the blast of cold numbed my armpit. "Turn around."

Turning, I squeezed my eyes shut as icy spray splashed my face. Darrell scrubbed and scrubbed; my body seemed to be freezing and reviving at the same time. "Open your coat," he said, and I robotically pulled apart the snaps of the slob-covered "blubber clothes."

In the head, a look at myself in the mirror revealed what I suspected, a blood-speckled, brown face with cracked, bleeding lips. I had felt them peeling half the day. Salty tear-tracks crisscrossed my cheekbones. My face burned. Both my hands were crusted with dried blood up past my wrists. I wondered how much of it was my own. After a harsh scrubbing in soapy hot water, some of it was gone. My fingernails harboured small beds of it but the thought of sleeping with it wasn't revolting. To me the Hunt meant blood, gore, aches, pains, dangers, risks, slave labour, and bitter cold.

Tea was hot and plentiful in the galley, but conversation was at an all-time low. Nobody seemed to feel like talking; most of it had already been said. Everyone seemed to be thinking of the poor day.

On my way through the wheel-house, I paused for the news of the day. Perry was in his chair, reading the Bible, Rodney in the other, biting his fingernails. The radio was alive, bringing loud and clear the news of damaged hulls, descriptive weather reports and radio seals. I knew they'd be on the go tonight because it had been a good day for hunting. The sea that had smashed the pack preceded a storm that was scheduled to arrive tomorrow. "Security. Security. Security. Marine forecast issued by Environment Canada at 8 P.M. for Friday, April 11...gale and storm warnings issued for the northeast coast....Gale force easterlies, forty-five, gusting to fifty-five knots, mixed with rain and blowing snow...temperature zero." So much for a good day tomorrow. Depressed like the rest, I went below.

Paul was poisoned. Stripping off my shirt I heard him say "A great lot of money for fourteen hours' work. Thirty seals, shifted twice, pays nine dollars a man. Fourteen hours for nine measly dollars."

I performed the acrobatic moves necessary to crawl into my sleeping bag without incident, relishing the feeling of pulling it up over my shoulders.

"My son, don't count your money yet, because your ticket to this misery is the first five hundred," Darrell put in from his bunk.

"It's not going to be a good spring," Paul replied, rolling over and switching off his light. "We're a long ways from five hundred yet. And by the looks of things, we won't be doing much better tomorrow. We'll be lucky to get enough to eat."

Nobody rose for that fly. It just flitted there for a long time before the sound of ice rubbing the hull drove it off. We all knew we were not doing well and that it didn't take long for 180 boats to fill the quota. Technically, we could spend two weeks in this environment and not see another seal, ending up owing the owners four hundred bucks for the experience. Not a good thought to sleep on. But sleep we did, in a civil ice-field, sixty miles northeast off Long Point.

Friday, April 11

The assault continued before first light. Banged back to reality and opening my eyes, I saw Gerard going up the ladder. He was sitting in the captain's chair studying the dials and indicators when I escaped up the ladder a short time later. My demeanour dropped when I glanced through the snow-lashed windows at the faint glow to the east. "Wouldn't the sight of that turn your stomach?" I said, sitting in the rumble seat.

"It's supposed to clear up a little this afternoon," he replied, punching some buttons on the instrument panel. "At this speed, it'll take us that long to get up to where we were last night. We drifted five-and-one-half-miles in ten hours."

"Make my day, Gerard," I replied, shifting in the chair to let Paul pass.

"Four hundred today," he said, disgustedly, stopping to scratch himself and look around. "Forget it! Fourteen hours of uninterrupted misery is what we're getting today. It should be nice up in the rigging. Christ!" The hull struck a pan and we all hung on.

After a hearty breakfast came deck duty. Gerard was dressing when I went down the ladder to the engine room. The distinct smell of blubber saturated the heat radiating from the roaring diesel. I passed by him to my dressing area.

The process of getting dressed was a procedure I faced with resignation. Pulling on the layers and tucking them in, I knew that regardless of what I wore, I'd be freezing in less than thirty minutes.

A bead of sweat streaked down my neck, sending a shiver through me. The first one of the day. If only I'd get a dollar for each and every one that would shake me in the next fifteen hours. It wouldn't matter that there were no seals. Everyone except David and Rodney was expected to be ready on deck. David cleared away the dishes and Rodney did what Rodneys do. Reaching for my vest, hat, scarf and gloves, I scampered up the ladder to finish dressing in the companionway. Darrell was coming out of the head. "It's not Palm Beach out there this morning," he said.

"I know." I turned for the frosty handle and opened the door to confront the miseries and dangers that I knew were there in abundance, a lot more abundant than the seals to be sure.

It was barbarous. The wind, flecked with rain, attacked me before I had the door closed. I instinctively turned my back to the onslaught and feverishly zipped up my coat. Gerard was aft, checking things out. He was wearing his greasy rubber clothes.

Dreading it, I took mine from the hook inside the "rubber room" and laid them on the hatch cover. They were cold and stiff, reminding me of wallboard and they cracked and resisted my efforts to pull them on. By the time I had the coat on, the sweat trail down my back was a speedway for chills. I shivered.

The stiff suit resisted my efforts to walk, although it did shelter me from the harsh wind. The ice-field was tight but reluctantly gave us passage. The extent of my visibility was two hundred yards and all of it was chock-full of shifting, drizzle-shrouded ice. A skim covered the pathetic pile of pelts and meat. Huddling in the lee, waiting to go to work, I was cold already, after only twenty minutes.

Eventually Rodney came out with a .243 Remington and ammo. "Big ones," he said. I followed him up the ladder. "Fifteen degrees colder," I thought, walking forward into the eye-watering wind.

Two hundred yards ahead in the rain and drizzle, a couple dozen mature harps lounged together on the shrouded floes, oblivious to the weather and our approach. The old dogs were the first to raise their big, black heads and look inquisitively at us. Their fur was dull grey, high-lighted by a large patch of black on their backs in the shape of a saddle. At one hundred yards they became alert, some crawling with extreme agility, in their fat-rolling gait, to the very edge of the pan. It is here that a lot of them die. It seems they can't resist that last look back, as if to see the bullet coming.

Perry and Randy took aim. *Bang! Bang!* Two of the black heads dropped. Swiftly reloading, they aimed again. *Bang!* Ice exploded by another's nose and he drew back in alarm. *Bang!* The pan came alive in a flurry of moving fur and flying lead. The smell of burnt gunpowder drifted on the cutting wind, spent bullet casings clinked on deck. Another head dropped. Three, with their chins held close to the pan, scurried with amazing speed across the sheet and without hesitation, plunged, with a wave of the hind scutters, into the sea. One large old dog made the fatal mistake of stopping at the fringe of the pan for a look and a bullet exploded in his head, spilling a finger-thick fountain of blood into the sea. When the shooting stopped, all but five were gone.

In a plume of black smoke the dragger pounced on its prize. Everything was a big rush now. Hurry. Hurry. Hurry. As fast as you can. The old man can look intimidating there atop the bridge watching you. It seemed to me that he expected us to perform as if we had just come out of the locker room after half time, ten points ahead.

We prepared to bring them on board, as quickly and efficiently as possible. That meant jumping out and pulling them together so as to make it as easy as possible for the boat to get close enough to winch them aboard.

Gerard operated the winch controls, located near the hydraulic pipes. He gave me slack and I grabbed the large iron hook attached to the seventy-foot nylon boom-rope, coiling fifteen feet of it in my hand. Darrell grabbed a steel ringed hawser and a gaff to which were spliced five slips, made of one-quarter-inch steel cable. Handing Gerard the hook and coiled rope, I picked a gaff and prepared to go.

The dead seals came into view through the driving sleet and, at the same time, Darrell and I jumped. The mattress-sized sheets were rough and slippery. My boots slipped out from under me when I landed. If it hadn't been for a natural reaction of sticking in the gaff, I would have slammed to the hard crust. Regaining some degree of stability on the gently shifting sheet, I ventured one slippery boot forward. With the motion of the two-metre swells rolling beneath them, the pans were alive, grinding softly together, stretching slowly apart. I glanced to see Darrell jaunting along, hopping over the clumpers, skipping across the cracks and jumping across rents toward a corpse. I knew the trick was to have some speed so I sunk the tine of my gaff into the crust and pushed off towards the first watery edge. My timing was late and as my momentum brought me to the edge, I realized it. I could have made it if it hadn't been for the stiff blubber-clothes. I fell short only by inches, falling in up to my thighs.

I wasn't afraid, just extremely alert. When my boots hit the slob, I knew I'd make it because the sea was stretching the ice abroad. I'd have lots of time (five or six seconds), to pull myself out. I felt the granite edge of the pan strike my left knee. Realizing I was going to slip back into the drink, I threw my upper body forward. Consciously, I stuck the hook into the crust and the gaff held my weight as I knew it would. The sea was just starting to throw the pans together when I shoved up on the pan. Standing and shaking myself like a wet retriever, I was glad that my feet were still warm and dry. My forehead was steaming.

"Go get 'em, Mickey!" I heard Gerard shout from the deck. Shaking my head, I again pushed off. This time I had my speed up before the next crevice and I jumped it easily. Then it was on to the next and the next; hopping, skipping and vaulting just like Darrell.

When I jaunted past him, he was laboriously pulling a great big, dead dog-harp towards the boat, eyes cast on the ice. His coat was open and his head was bare. Skipping up to another harp, that lay quietly, spurting a fountain of steaming blood eight inches into the air, staining the pan, I stuck the hook of the gaff into the hole in his skull. I plucked on the slippery handle to turn him towards the ship, not having his big neck straightened out before I was down on my knees on the slippery, hard sheet. Out loud I snarled out verses of curses at the thing in reaction to the pain that shot through my body. The sound of my own voice frightened me. Even though I riddled the words, my voice sounded harsh and barbaric. The big old harp, the focus of my rage, just lay there staring at me with my gaff stuck to the side of his head.

Springing to my feet, I again stretched the bugger out. This time I was ready for his dead weight and I managed to turn him toward the waiting ship. He was heavy, every bit of five hundred pounds. Ahead, across the fluctuating floes, I saw that Darrell had his tow lying on a flat sheet and he was heading in the direction of another. To his pan was where I headed, the dead brute dragging behind me. At the edge of each shifting piece, I'd stop and pull the seal beside me, then jump across the gap onto the next rocking pan. Then, I'd turn and pull the seal across behind me. The monster would slide into the sea and it was all I could do to pull him back out. Sweating profusely, my rubber jacket wide open catching the icy wind, I finally finished my tow. The boat bashed its way alongside.

"Heads up!" I heard Gerard call just before the hook struck me in the back. The impact numbed my body and piled me atop the two dead dogs. I emitted just a small bit of blasphemy a few decibels lower than the roar of the Volvo. "Sorry about that, Mick, boy," I heard Gerard apologize to my bent, paining back.

"That's alright, you didn't try, did you?"

"No sir! I wouldn't strike you in the back on purpose."

Straightening up, rubbing my back and arching my body, I replied, "I believe you, Gerard."

Grabbing the steel hawser, I bottled the misery I felt and bent to place the steel slips over a rear flipper of both dead dogs. Perry watched and waited. Reaching for the cursed hook, I put it through the eye ring. Holding the slips tightly on the flippers, I gave the signal, Gerard engaged the winch and they were both pulled, none too gracefully, spraying blood and salt water, in over the rail onto the deck.

Darrell was coming toward me with his second tow. Grabbing my gaff I went for another. By the time I got back with it and those two had been winched in, Darrell was coming with the last one. "This one's a dirty bitch," he scowled in disgust. I swore aloud on the cursed thing.

"You killed a bitch, skipper!" Darrell shouted at the bridge.

Looking up I saw Perry looking back down. "I didn't. Randy did," came the response.

"Bring it aboard anyway. It's better than nothing," Randy bellowed.

Darrell didn't answer aloud. In a cold voice, comparable only to the heat-sucking wind that charged inside my opened coat, I heard him grate, "Well, Randy. You can come down and pelt this now!" We followed the tow aboard.

Back on deck, watching the blood pan fall away astern and feeling the sweat stream down my neck, I got to thinking about death in the floes. When I'm out here, even with a crowd of men, I am alone. I may be able to look across the rising and falling distances and find some degree of comfort in the fact that I am "right alongside," but in reality a man would have to be a lot closer to help out. The longest a sealer is in the water is seven seconds before the crush comes on. I could be up to my waist thrashing in the slob. Whatever part of me submerged wouldn't ever be the same. I'd call for help and slip beneath the pan, more than likely helpless on account of just having had the life squashed out of me. I can't hear. I can't see. The ice goes abroad again, and slob fills in all the spaces. The tide has taken me or the pan has pushed me down. All that there is to indicate I was even there is my hat. It is plucked from the slob with a gaff, to give to my wife and family. It's as simple as that. Sealers earn their meagre pay.

Randy didn't pelt the dirty thing. I did. Pelting mature seals is different from pelting young seals. Four times bigger makes four times harder. Four times as much hot, reeking blood, four times as much pungent, rising steam. Four times as heavy, four times as revolting. With only five aboard and no rush, the three of us did one seal at a time. Gerard made the first decisive six-foot slash, exposing the ribcage. Fine, thin geysers of blood sprayed from pinhole punctures made by the knife. These liberally sprayed our clothes and sometimes our face. I worked the hind half, slicing the two-inch-thick layer of fat from the ribcage and rear flippers while Gerard worked around the head and shoulders. Kneeling in the swath, I prepared to relieve the big dog of his penis.

It was a gruesome, despicable minute's work. After carefully slicing the skin along beside the eight-inch bone, I reached with my hand and seized it. Pulling it off from the pelvis, I carefully cut away the membrane attaching it. Placing both hands on the handle of my slippery knife, I applied maximum pressure with the tip of my blade to an area two inches up the pelvic bone. This was the dangerous part. If the hull lurched or glanced off a sheet at that moment, it was easy for my hand to slip down across the sharp blade. Once the bone was severed it was easy to finish the job by carefully cutting away all clinging flesh. Care must be taken not to cut the thing. When a last slash freed it from the bone, I tossed it into a special "dick-pan." Bending again, I located the right testicle and, careful not to slice it, freed it from its sac. Tossing it in with the penis, I bent again to remove the other, tossing it into the tub. When the pelt lay flat on the deck, Darrell stuck the tine of a long meat-hook in the twitching monstrosity. Using the hook, he pulled the carcass over allowing me to sculp the pelt from the backbone. He then dragged the steaming body astern, using the axe to chop open the ribcage. Reaching down, he grabbed the windpipe, slashing it with his knife. Pulling on it, he didn't straighten again until he had the steaming, dripping network of organs dangling in his hands. Gerard bent to extricate the left shoulder; I bent for the right. I tossed mine in the tub; his fell short. He grabbed the two hundred pound pelt by the eye holes, dragging it, slip-sliding, astern for washing. I picked up the flipper, threw it in a tub and rolled another one onto the gory spot. The other three watched me hone my knife with fixed gazes. One of the bitch's eyes was hanging out on her cheek. We repeated the process.

An old dog organ, as every sealer knows, brings the best kind of money. Last year, on our first trip, we had brought in 550, almost a large fish containerful. Very discreetly, they were loaded onto a pick-up that disappeared in the night. We received more money from that tub of organs then we did from a tractor-trailer loaded with pelts, meat and fat. Asians loved them. Nothing less then six inches was acceptable. They averaged seventy dollars each and we only had to handle them twice.

Before I put the blade to the bitch's chest, I called to Randy to come down. He stiffly turned his whole body in my direction, giving me the signs that he did not hear what I said. Waving my bloody knife at him, I pointed to the bitch. He understood immediately, responding by making a "waving away" gesture with his left arm before turning his gaze forward. Gerard worked the front, I worked the rear in the blood and gore and milk. It was as revolting a spectacle as ever I saw. "Jesus Christ! How much is this worth an hour?" I said turning away to look for a spell at the passing floe so white and pure and clean.

"This is not worth nothing!" Darrell fumed in the steam. "Might get fifty cents a man for it by the time we gets it on the truck." He spit over the rail.

Gerard didn't say anything. Slowly, carefully, he went to the rail and, without bending, he was sick over the side. With eyes watering, not uttering a word, he returned to his place, bent over and started to relieve the bitch of its shoulder. I swore I'd never eat anything "strawberry" again.

We weren't finished with them yet. Each carcass had to be decapitated and de-flippered. Also, these big carcasses were each chopped into four smaller pieces to allow for easier handling, and stowing. Gruesome work. Often, I'd find myself kneeling on the gory deck, face spattered with specks of blood and meat, surrounded by the black, hateful looking things, with a blood-dripping axe held in one hand, a decapitated head with glassy eyeballs intact held in the other. The hull would strike a pan and the pile would slither down, covering my lap. Sometimes, during those sickening times, I'd stop, look up at the sky and realize what I was doing. What had I become? "What a man wouldn't do for a buck or two," I'd say to myself, taking in a lungful of air (sometimes it would be more oily smoke than air), exhale a gush of steam, look back down, grab a greasy ribcage, struggle it across the bloody, meat-engrained chopping block and viciously decapitate the body. The word "barbaric" would flash through my mind and it would set off a litany of thoughts that always thundered the same way.

I had heard the anti-sealing protesters say that sealers were barbarians. They were right. You have to be a barbarian to survive it! However, it wasn't barbaric to the seals. They were on a picnic. Everything else is barbaric. How barbaric one became depended on how long one was subjected to it. Once, after only a short time into the Hunt, I had saved up ten heads that we used for two hours to play "head-ball." It was like hockey but instead of using sticks, we used our hakipiks to try to shoot the head between two twitching carcasses we used as goal-posts. We all took turns in the net. By the time the game was over, eyeballs, teeth, fragments of skull bone and lower jawbones were scattered all over the rink. Darrell won but we all had a great bit of fun.

Soon they were cooling on the stern. In the lee of the superstructure, holding the hot pipes, I waited for the rifle to fire. The lazy arctic wind cut through me unabated, at forty, gusting to fifty-five, knots. I worked stiffly around the deck, my slob-coated blubber clothes resisting me every step of the way. I reached to put up my hood to stop a pang of cold from stabbing the back of my neck, racing for the marrow of my bones. I hunched my shoulders to impede its progress and I found that my hood was already up. The hull stopped. *Bang! Bang! Bang! Bang!* "Over the side, Mickey."

At 9:30 A.M., shrivelled with cold, I had the first flash of the comfort of my bunk. We had twelve old dogs sculpted and they were crowding yesterday's catch. Before stowing them below decks in the pounds, we needed ice and we knew where to get plenty of that.

Rodney stopped beside a raftered pan and Darrell and I jumped off with axes. Chopping chunks from the tangles, we filled up the net-bag. "Too bad this stuff is not worth a dollar a pound," I said, struggling to get the heavy clump into the bag.

"My son, if this stuff was worth a dollar a pound, the Norwegians would be over here and have it all brought home. We wouldn't be allowed to take a cube," Darrell responded making a vicious chop at a ledge, that sprayed ice inside my coat.

Gerard pulled it in with the winch and dumped it on deck. "Yes sir, yes sir, three bags full," and we followed the sling back aboard. With a puff of black smoke, the ship lurched ahead.

I knelt amongst the chunks and with the back of the axe, smashed the pieces into small fragments. The hatch cover was removed and yesterday's pathetic catch of thirty carcasses and pelts were tossed down. It took Darrell no more than twenty minutes to lift, shift, stow and ice them in their pounds. Emerging from the hold in a bath of sweat specked with blood, he went straight for the rail, opening his coat as he went. After we had put the hatch-cover back in place it was "wash-down" time. The hose blasted icy cold water all over me while I got a sound rubbing with the brush from Darrell. I was perished again, finding a little comfort holding on to the warm hydraulic lines. Then I wanted to pee.

The thought of it caused a pang of dread to course through my chilled body. The last thing I wanted to do was expose myself to the arctic. That was where my last reserves of heat were stored. I immediately nipped it at the bud.

As the minutes dragged by the urge increased and I resigned myself to the fact that the gauntlet must be run. I took off my greasy, bloody gloves and headed for the rail. My cold hands reached for the sticky clasps and I opened up to the elements. A sharp gust blasted right through me when I reached to unclasp the pants, pushing them down. Dreading it every inch of the way, I compressed my muscles and gritted my teeth when the wind attacked my naked flesh. *Brrrrrr.*

By the time I was finished, my vitals, my hands and face, were all the one numb temperature. I realized I'd rushed it a little when I felt liquid warmth heat a spot on my leg. The warmth was quickly snuffed out by the chill and before I had my coat buttoned up, it had turned into an extra-cold spot next to my skin. I was beginning to hate this, again. We had just finished our ablution when the boat stopped. *Bang! Bang!* "Over the side, Mickey."

"You're a slave-driver, Gerard."

So the dreary morning dragged on. Time seemed to drip by like the melting of a giant iceberg. The seals were scarce, the reports of the rifle fewer and further between. The weather deteriorated from barbaric to intolerable. "I'm going in for a cup of tea," I said to no one in particular as we huddled together. "I'm just about petrified here. I stands all I can stands, I can't stands no more."

"I'm coming right behind you," Darrell said, shucking his woolen gloves and going for the hasps on his rubber jacket.

"What time is it, Darrell?" I asked, pulling off my own gloves and hanging them on the hot pipes.

"It's now 9:15," he declared, holding onto Gerard's shoulder, struggling to get the slippery pants over the heel of his boot.

"That's not all it is!" I exclaimed, figuring it must be at least dinner time. "Do you mean this day is only three hours old! My God! We've got another eleven hours of this!"

"Eleven hours in this day. At the rate they're coming aboard, we'll have days like this until June."

"Perish the thought," I said, stiffly reaching for the greasy clasps of my jacket. As I forced it to comply, it cracked and buckled. The thought of pulling it all on again did nothing to lift my spirits.

The heat in the engine room revived me. The tea was hot and revitalizing but the thought of going back into the freezer took the pleasure from my brief repose. Darrell tried his best to cheer me but failed.

Through the dressing procedure, various things played on my mind: the holding on, the lurching of the hull, ice-pans scrunching past, sweat which I knew would be a crust of ice in a very few minutes. My good hooded sweater was now good only for the garbage. Blood was crusted and dried halfway up the arms so I took a knife and cut the sleeves off at the elbows, using the rag to clean some blood off the floor. My good winter coat was in the same sad state of gore but

I left it as it was. I reached for my garbage hat, gloves, and scarf and cautiously scampered up the ladder to escape the stifling heat. The awareness that it was not yet 10:00 A.M. took the good out of me. All the while I was dressing, I heard only one shot. It was going to be a long, hard day with no pay. *What am I doing here?* I opened the door and stepped out into the freezer.

It was as I expected; my heat was gone and the sweat had chilled me before I finished battling into my blubber clothes. It was like I had never warmed up at all.

Bang! Bang! "Over the side, Mickey."

By 2:00 P.M. it wasn't fit for an old harp to pup. Visibility was down to a bleak fifty yards, howling wind whipping the snow and driving it in a low drift. We all agreed that it was not fit to be out and none of us knew why we were. Thirty pathetic pelts lay on the aft deck and the sight of them plunged us deeper into despair.

By 4:00 P.M. the weather worsened to the point where it became impossible to navigate due to near zero visibility, gale-force winds, slop-snow, sleet, and drizzle. Perry came down saying that was it for now. We had forty-five cooling at the time. We were all eager to get in out of it and we filed in to wash and warm ourselves.

After ten minutes in the heat of the engine room, I was revived enough to drink tea and eat a light lunch. I was glad to be in looking out at the blusterous northeast winds and driving snow.

The comfort was short-lived however, when at 5:30 P.M. the Volvo fired to life and I was once again summoned to the open deck. The skipper said it had cleared a little but I hadn't noticed any improvement. I was huddled at the time I heard the shot. David looked at me saying, "He's my puppy, now."

I watched him. He jumped and on impact with the icy surface, slipped and fell heavily. Getting up slowly, he crippled on to retrieve the young harp. Back aboard he told us he had twisted his ankle and hurt his elbow. I stiffly steeled my knife and sculped the harp, barely warming myself up.

Bang! Bang! David limped over to get his gaff while the ship battled forward, waging her war against a barely relenting foe. He braced himself for the jump and sprang from the rails. Watching him as he landed, I saw him sink in the snow to the depth of his calves and he fell forward in a clump. Agony showed on his face and he gave out a yelp. Grinding his teeth, he tried to stand up.

Darrell jumped and landed beside him and helped him back to the rail. We assisted him over, evidently in great pain. Darrell ran on to get the tow, David hobbled around looking more and more like an old man. "No more on ice for you, today," Perry said to him. "Go inside until you feel better." David crippled around for another spell before we helped him out of his clothes.

At 8:00 P.M. the Hunt stopped for the night and we were all glad to close the door for the last time on the miserable day. Three hours of misery had seen five seals come in over the rail, one every thirty-six, freezing minutes.

I was glad to crawl into bunk around 9:30 P.M. David moaned and groaned as he painfully crawled into his berth. "I know I'll get in," he said, in a grimace, "I just don't think I'll be able to get back out." I wanted to laugh but it was no laughing matter.

The winds huffed and the snow swirled. We were all waiting for it. "Security. Security. Security. Marine weather forecast issued by...for Saturday...Funk Island Bank...storm force north-easterlies...forty-five, gusting to sixty knots...snow and blowing snow...temperatures minus ten...highs two degrees...."

"Oh, God," I muttered. The others pretended they didn't hear.

SATURDAY, APRIL 12

I got little sleep. The swell always heaves before the wind and before long I felt the effects of it. Beethoven haunted the hull all night banging to get in. He tried the bow, he tried the stern, he attacked the port and the starboard. All night he persisted, knocking, banging, grinding his teeth inches from my ear, causing me to twist and turn, moan and groan, roll and crouch. What didn't pain ached, burned, throbbed, spasmed, twitched or stung. I couldn't bear to touch my knees together because they were too tender. I couldn't get warm. Shiver after shiver kept me mostly in the fetal position. Thinking back over the course of the day, I figured my body had boiled and frozen at least seventy times. I remembered the forecast: forty-five to sixty...."

"Sixty." That was the number of pelts Perry reported that evening on the radio. Not too proudly I might add. He blamed it on the elements like everyone else who didn't fare well. Sixty pelts. The pay structure for sealers worked out to approximately eight cents each for every seal that comes in over the rail. Add to that eight cents a sealer for each time a seal is shifted. Before it's finally loaded in the truck, we will have moved it about twelve times. That makes ninety-six cents a seal. Lying on deck cooling, they are worth thirty cents each. Today's thirteen barbaric hours had netted me eighteen dollars. I came to this realization with a groan. My mouth was parched, my tongue thick and dry. I could barely swallow. Eighteen dollars. That wouldn't pay for the soap to clean the stink of blubber off my sore body...forty-five, gusting to sixty knots.... *Thump!* Some things are worse than dying. A part of me would have been relieved to see the dripping edge of the pan thundering towards my bunk. It didn't. But it did cause David to reel back in his sleep, gasp out in pain and curse a few venomous oaths before painfully settling back. Misery loves company.

The Volvo fired to life at 6:00 A.M., followed by Gerard, scampering up the ladder like he was abandoning ship, switching on lights along the way. I clung on for a few more minutes. It was *crash, bang, whop, whip, lurch, slam, stop, go astern, vrooom!* (brace myself), *vibrate, shimmy, whoosh, tinkle, crash, lurch, rock, shiver, shudder, shake, rattle and roll* all to the crescendo of *ice crunching, ice banging, ice rising, ice tipping over, ice sinking; beside me* (bless myself), *behind me, above me, below me, on the counter, on the stem, on the stern, amidships, aft, forward and reverse.*

Paul snarled out in a rage. "By Jesus I'm beat to pieces!" he started. "This is the worst beating I ever took without getting in a few smacks!" He had one leg in his jogging pants, lifting his other leg over the waistband when the hull lurched to starboard and to port he went. Roaring out in surprise and pain, he slid downward, his face reflecting aggravated agony when it passed down inches from mine. The top of his curly head dropped from my view and, rolling to the outside edge of my bunk, I looked down to see him atop the luggage, rubbing his knee with one hand, the side of his face with the other, his joggers in a tangle around his ankles.

Pulling the sleeping bag over my head, I laughed to kill myself. I couldn't help it. The image of his face passing along in front of mine cracked me up. My guts hurt and I strained myself to keep as quiet as I could. A few moments later, under control (to a point), I flung back the bag, almost about to burst again at the thought, but I managed to ask him if he was all right.

"No!" came the snarl. "I'll never be all right again!"

"What part hurts the most?" I asked, wiping tears off my cheeks.

"All of me hurts. Honest to God, I'm afraid to get up and I'm afraid to stay down."

I laughed out loud at that. So did Randy. "I thought you was `killed!" he giggled.

"Don't laugh! Yer not up yet! Oooohhh."

He got a couple of good knocks out of it. Three or four lurches later, Darrell, as fluid as a wave, hardly staggering in the onslaught, pulled on tight jeans, socks, T-shirt, wool sweater and two sneakers in jig time without mishap. "How are you feeling David?" he asked looking right at him.

"If I can survive this, never again will I be out here!" came the growl.

"That good, eh?"

"What's so good about that?"

"At least you got hopes of getting in. By the way, Perry is whopping it to her this morning, I got little hopes of us being afloat much longer." David just groaned and tried to turn over. He couldn't. *Whop! Lurch! Crunch! Bang!* Darrell was gone.

Randy was out next. Shaking the black, tangled mop of hair on his head, his face still asleep, he repeated over and over, "Boys, oh boys, oh boys, oh boys!" The ship tried to shake him awake but he was awake enough to hold on tightly. "Oh boys, oh boys, oh boys," all the way up the ladder.

Paul tried again while Perry shifted the tranny from astern to "maximum-full" ahead. His joggers pulled up tightly, he scampered up the ladder with his sneakers, socks, and shirt in his hand, not looking back once, just up and gone.

That left David and me alone in the ricochet room. During the moments we stopped dead, I could hear the wind howling. "Gusting to sixty…" Humour had deserted me. Fourteen hours out in that certainly wasn't funny. I noticed a salty wetness on my cheek. I wondered what kind of teardrop it was.

I knew David wasn't getting up; he couldn't. All he could do was hold on, wince and bear it. Reluctantly reaching out, I grabbed what I had to wear, and pulled it all in beside me. Woefully pushing back the warm cover, I heavy-heartedly dressed in my coffin. "Jesus Christ grant me the endurance." I waited my chance, consciously bracing and blessing myself against the violence and turbulence dead ahead.

It wasn't as bad as I feared, or was I just getting "barbarian-ized?" I opened the watertight door, grinding my teeth in expectation. It was a full hour before I had to take up position at the hot pipes. Shelter from the snow-spitting wind was as scarce as the seals. There was nothing black within the five hundred yards of white that I could make out. There was just some green and gray where the sea and wind were ripping the ice-field to pieces and a long, green, serpent of it astern. The snowflakes were small and wet and stuck to our shiny blubber clothes. The swells had swollen in the night, consistently advancing, three metres high and seven seconds apart. They effortlessly bench-pressed tens of millions of tons of ice all around me. The crusty pans bobbed and tipped in the swells, one taking a dipping, the other a dripping. The sea had eaten them away at their water lines, causing them to be top-heavy. This was dangerous ice for the jumper. Not only is a pan apt to capsize, the lip can easily founder with the added weight of man and tow.

I thought it must have been 11:00 P.M. when the first bullet exploded inside a skull. I was clinging onto the pipes, exposed to the elements, thinking of something to think about to stop me from shivering when I heard the words, "Over the side, Mickey." I thought it was just a dream at first. My mind and gaze had frozen in the swirling of the snows and the pitching of the floes. Jolted back to reality my mind screamed, "You're not going out there!" Selecting a gaff, I waited for the fish-eater to show through the blur.

David stayed in bunk; there wasn't any point of his being up, although he said that his back was a little better. To me he didn't look too good. Gerard never left the deck. He was short and heavy and although he was consistent, he wasn't spry. Darrell didn't like to jump and avoided it every chance he got. "There's a feeling that comes over me when I leave the rails that I can't handle," he said. "I hates it!"

Paul, jumper number two, owned the only survival suit aboard and he well needed it where he spent most of the brutal hours: high in the rigging spotting for seals and leads. Randy spent most of his time on the wheel-house, huddled in the lee of the control booth. We weren't sure what he was supposed to be but we knew he didn't want anything to do with anything that could get blood on him. He spelled the gunner, he spelled the navigator, he operated the speedboat but very seldom did he help us.

Rodney was the skipper's son. He didn't have to pelt or jump or drag or stow or wash dishes. He steered the boat, slouched in the chair and wore a long face, having most to say to Perry.

Perry wasn't going to jump. He was captain. David, jumper number one, was in "sick-bay." He couldn't stand up, much less jump. That left me number-one jumper. I selected a gaff and stuck my head out around the corner to spot my tow. Wind lashed me, ice stung me. It snatched the air from my lower stomach, blasting it full again with a cold, burning blast that made my eyelids close and my eyeballs water. Blurry-eyed and thoroughly chilled, I withdrew to the huddle. "Jesus," I prayed aloud. "I don't have to go out in that do I?"

Darrel heard what I said. "What's the matter Mickey, getting cold feet?"

"Cold feet!" I echoed, "If that was all that was cold, I'd be laughing." He said something to me as I let go the rail but the wind swallowed it before it reached my ears. They were filled with the sound of ice crunching on fiberglass.

I didn't mind it once I got into it. In fact, at times it was invigorating. The crust was hard, the heels of my boots scrunched in with every hop, skip, jump, vault, stop and go I made. The beaters slid easily behind me and the rail was always there within arm's reach whenever I stretched for it to climb aboard. I didn't mind the sweat, I didn't mind the oily fumes, I wasn't repulsed by the gore and the day seemed to be brightening up a trifle. Darrell and Gerard seemed to be in good spirits as well. Often during the wait for the report of the rifle, we'd sing a few songs, tell a few jokes or just huddle together watching the teeter-tottering floes together. The smell of spent gunpowder stimulated me, the blasting arctic wind freshened me and the sight of blood excited me. This was the Hunt.

Everything was done quickly; you snatched the seal as fast as you could, then charged on to the next and the next and the next, one at a time.

Every jump is different and one caused me a wetting. Returning with my tow, I had stopped, momentarily, for the pans to throw together. A ledge I was standing on collapsed under my feet, immersing me into the frigid water up to my thighs before my gaff stopped my plunge. My heart was in my mouth when I finally pulled myself out. I continued with my tow and made it back aboard just as I felt the pang of cold trickle into my boots. I was wet.

It was then I realized that although I had thought I was freezing before, I wasn't. This was freezing. The pang of death oozed through my socks, numbing my feet and toes.

"Did you get wet?" Darrell asked, positioning the seal, on its back, between his feet.

"Yes," I replied.

"Then go below and change as quick as you can. Get a cup of hot tea while you're at it."

I didn't want to do that. I had to strip down and re-dress. That was a gauntlet in itself and the thought was demoralizing, but the water was excruciatingly cold. I tried to move my toes, feeling nothing. I resigned myself to it. It was 9:30 A.M.

In the engine room, I hung my wet socks and clothes in the heat. My long underwear was wet to the knees, my wet skin took on a blue cast. I sat atop a bucket and warmed up beside the roaring engine. When sweat beads formed on my brow, I went for dry clothes. I felt like crawling into bunk but I knew it was to be a long, arduous, miserable ten hours more before I felt the warmth of the sleeping bag surround me. David turned over, groaning, asking me what had happened. I helped him get out of bed and steadied him while he climbed up the ladder, thinking, "No on-ice for you today, either." I drank a cup of steaming tea, watching him trying to function; each lurch of the hull caused him to wince in pain.

"Go back to bed, David. There's nothing you can do with a bad back."

"There's no comfort there. I'm beat from dog to devil. I'm getting dressed and coming out."

"Misery loves company," I replied, washing my mug and putting it back in the cupboard. "But just remember, if you twist your back again, you might end up in a wheelchair." He didn't reply; the cabin shifted and his face twisted into a snarl of agony.

Back on deck, wearing a plastic bag inside my wet boot to keep the liner from sogging my socks, I noticed that the weather was clearing up and the action was picking up. As the day got warmer, the seals started crawling from the water to lounge and digest on the pans. On miserable, stormy days they stayed below. In jig time, "jumper number one" was in full swing. Gerard kindly reminded me once in a while, when after the report of the rifle he'd grin at me and say, "Over the side, Mickey."

"You're a slave-driver, Gerard." At noon I got ready for jump number thirty-five. It was hard, dangerous work and my body was feeling the effects of it. My ankles hurt from the impact with the ice pans, my shoulders throbbed from the exertion of pulling them around. My legs ached and the first thoughts of being "too old for this" surfaced in my head.

The ice-field split abroad with the wind and tide and conditions improved enough for the speedboat to work. "Do you mind if Paul uses your rifle?" Perry asked.

"No, not a bit," I replied. A lifejacket was secured with rope to the cuddy; ammunition, flares, gas, radio, food and drinks were stowed, then we hoisted it over the rail. Randy started the sixty horsepower Enduro and I slipped their painter, saying, "Shoot to kill, show no mercy, take no prisoners and the best of luck."

"Steer to the northeast," the skipper said, returning to the gunning table. The boys disappeared into the floes.

We hunted away the time and by two o'clock, I had made my fiftieth jump. By this time everything hurt and I had to summon my reserves to get back safely. The ice had gotten rotten in the last while and to jump now meant landing six inches deep in the rotting crust. This sinking feeling was very frightening because I felt like I was going to pass right through and disappear under the floes, never again to see the light of day. Butterflies fluttered in my churning stomach and my heart was in my throat each and every time I jumped.

They weren't all clean kills. Not all lay deathly still, quietly fountaining a finger of steaming blood. Some were very much alive when I reached them. They got it with the gaff. Some came to life on deck, lifting their heads, looking around through eyes of swirling blood. Some just lay quietly, trying to hide the glimmer of life that glowed within them. These got the hakipik as soon as they were discovered.

As I sat on the rail after jump number sixty, breathing hard, sweating and shivering, the thought that I was too old for the Hunt resurfaced. I was almost exhausted. No one volunteered to take a turn, all were hard at work...roll the seal over on its back, bend, make the initial cut. Slash, grab, lift, pull...toss it over the side. Darrell cut out the heart of one fresh harp and placed it on the Coleman. It throbbed and pumped for three minutes before it lay still. We would keep the hearts and livers in a bucket to bring home when the voyage was over. I knew that even as appalling as the dirty stuff looked now, baked in a roaster, adorned with vegetables, it was a feast fit for a king.

At number eighty, I began to hate those words, "Over the side, Mickey." They came so easily from Gerard's mouth. I didn't care if the ice could support my weight or not. I did the work in a robotic fashion, my muscles surprising me each time I managed to laboriously leap the leads, jump the rents and climb in over the rails. I felt impervious to the cold and danger. It was a burden just to carry my gaff. On more than a couple of occasions, I envied the heavy dead harps I dragged behind me. They had it over with.

At 5:00 P.M. the speedboat returned with forty-five seals and we promptly hoisted them aboard. Extra gas and ammo was stowed aboard and they disappeared again. "Shoot to kill, take no prisoners, good luck."

I warmed a little as I helped pelt between the rifle reports.

Continuous labour had the benefit of producing heat and my body revived somewhat in the hot blood and steaming carcasses. We continued our assault, worming our way left and right, belching clouds of black, oily, soot and smoke that smeared my face and coated my lungs.

Bang! Bang! I left the half-pelted seal and prepared for jump number one hundred. I saw the dead harp four swells away across the rotting, shifting ice pans. Blessing and bracing myself, I picked a spot to land.

If I went through the pan the misery would be over in two or three minutes and, the way I felt, that would be a blessing. All feelings of fear and apprehension were frozen inside me and I skipped from pan to pan, claimed the dead harp and dragged it back. More often than not the fish-eater didn't go cleanly in over the rail. Because I was tiring, my efforts were often wasted and the seal splashed back into the water. Gerard would wait for me to drag myself aboard and together we'd pull the ninety-pounder five feet straight up, then pull him in over the rails. Sometimes, we'd have the bloody thing to the gunnels and the gaff would tear out. It would drop back into the sea and we'd hook it again and pull it in.

At 7:00 p.m., with the winds spitting snow, the speedboat returned deep in the rubble with sixty. Paul and Randy looked cold and relieved when we made the painter fast.

"That will be all for the speedboat today," Perry said. "Tie her tight to the stern and we'll load it when we stop for the night." The seals made a great pile and we started in to clean them up. Rodney gunned the engine and the hull sprang ahead.

I jumped another twenty times in the next hour, adding fresh ones to the heaping pile. "How much is this worth an hour? Come on, dark!" A pile of dirty pelts lay beside a steaming heap of freshly butchered carcasses, not yet decapitated. They stared at me grotesquely when I a tossed a fresh, twitching atop the pile. *Bang! Bang!* "Over the side." Put my knife down, pick up my gaff, get ready.

My blubber clothes were filthy, my face was spattered, and my body ached at every move. *Bang!* I was ten times more sore than I was sorry when, at last darkness came. The lights in the spar glared on and we stopped in the pack. The harps had all deserted the floes to spend the night searching for and destroying our fish. Under the glare I endured the numbing wash-down and got ready for the cooked supper David had somehow prepared for us.

10:00 P.M. found me again knee-deep in gore. Select one from the pile, place it between my feet, bend, slash, reach, pull, slurp, toss it to the wind. Take a look around. Bend, slash, puncture, plunge my fingers in. Lift, cut, slash, straighten, shift, bend, grab, slash, blood geysering, spraying, sloshing, throw it in the tub. Shift, bend, slip, slide, in the steam, in the cold, in the night, just like Darrell, Gerard and Paul.

Sunday, April 13

It was past midnight before we had them all sculpted, decapitated, washed, scrubbed, cleaned, and stowed. We loaded the speedboat, washed, scrubbed, and readied it, and scrubbed the deck and ourselves.

Exhausted and cold, I passively endured the wash-down, my skeleton rattling freely as the frigid water sprayed me and Darrell scrubbed me, my mind thinking of the sleeping bag. Gerard helped me out of my blubber clothes. The zipper of my heavy coat was frozen with ice and blood and I couldn't pull it down. I asked Paul to help me. He grabbed it, pulled, and the zipper broke. Horrified, I realized my coat was ruined.

"Sorry about that," he said, pulling away from me.

"You're sorry!" I said, sarcastically. "Not half as sorry as I'll be tomorrow when I have to work in this freezing hell wearing a coat with no zipper!"

"I didn't try to do it, it was frozen solid. Do you have another coat?"

"Paul, if I was well enough off to be able to afford two winter coats, I wouldn't be out here!" I turned for the engine room to shuck my clothes and hang them to dry. My coat was ruined. That was a very serious setback and I had nothing to replace it. My heart sunk in my frozen stomach.

I was in no mood for eating. I washed up and headed for the bunk but found no comfort there. I twisted and turned from my aches and pains. It hurt to touch my knees together, my arms throbbed wherever I placed them. I wasn't in good shape. I had jumped 154 times in the last fourteen hours, dragging back a seal that weighed almost as much as I did each and every time. How many miles and how many pounds was that? And that wasn't dragging on a hockey rink. I swore I'd never do it again. I knew my body couldn't stand it and, besides, it wasn't worth it. All tallied, we had 330 seals aboard, another 170 before I made a cent and now I didn't have a coat to wear. I moaned, realizing I had made the turn without having to pull my sleeping bag off my shoulder. I knew the weight was falling off me. At least four pounds gone. I let out a sigh, drew up in a fetal position and succumbed, dreading the oncoming day. I searched my mind for the positive aspects of this expedition and found none. I got comfort only from the fact that this was to be my last Hunt.

Aches, throbs, and spasms of pain kept me tossing all night. I dragged seals, pulled and strained, slipped and fell. I was submerged beneath the floes and came out of my sleep in a frenzy, coated with a lather of sweat. Beethoven played all night long.

At 5:00 A.M., Perry gave us the wake-up call, "Come on, boys, put down the fat." I dreaded this time, shrinking into my sleeping bag, knowing what was in store. I eventually moaned and groaned my way out and laboriously pulled on my clothes. My guts were too sore and shrunken to accept food but I forced down an egg and some toast, then to the engine room. I passively accepted the heat and sweat as it trickled down my back and brow when I pulled on my blood-crusted outer wear and lined boots. Pathetically, I tried to fix the zipper of my coat with a pair of pliers but succeeded only in breaking it in two pieces. I had to wear it anyway.

It was a bitter 5:30 A.M. when I opened the door and met the arctic morning. It felt like forty below when I pulled on my crispy blubber clothes. As expected, the sweat froze to my skin. The dawn was but a hint in the frozen eastern horizon when we started work under the mast floodlights.

Darrell and Paul lifted the hatch-cover of the hold and

disappeared below. Gerard, Randy and I started throwing down the pelts. I walked to the stern where they were tiered, fat up. Reaching down, I drove my hand into a flipper hole. The pelt was greasy and cold and weighed fifty pounds. Taking the weight of it and turning, I bent for another. Grasping one in each hand, I dragged them across the greasy deck to the hold. Lifting them one at a time over the two-foot lip, I dropped them into the centre pound atop the ice, eight feet below. Gerard and Randy did the same and we made up a procession back and forth.

The constant work massaged my sore and aching body and I soon began to warm up. I felt better dragging the pelts over and the sun, in a blaze of glory, rose out of the frozen, jagged ice-field.

Perry fired up the main engine and soon we were ricocheting and worming our way to the northeast. The deck became slimy and slippery. We dragged the pelts to the hold and once the hull skidded out from under me, leaving me in a pile, striking my sore elbows and banging my aching knees. I didn't swear. I was resigned to the misery and I absorbed the knocks, bangs, strains and pains as they came. This was my last Hunt. Never again.

Finally the last pelts were tossed down. Three hundred carcasses and six hundred flippers remained, frozen in a revolting clump of tangled, black meat. The pelts were slippery and heavy; the meat was cold, bloody and repulsive.

Kneeling beside Randy in the midst of the pile, I reached for the first one. Driving my fingers into the hole in the ribcage, I plucked it from the heap and tossed it toward the hatch where Gerard stood waiting for Darrell and Paul to finish stowing. Digging deeper and deeper into the pile of gross-looking things, I found myself knee-deep in blood and black meat. "Hold up for a few minutes. Give the boys a chance to move the pelts."

Kneeling there, I watched the sun rising low on the horizon, veiled in a cloud of frost. Fingers of gold pointed towards fluffy clouds frozen to a clear-blue sky. None of its rays touched me, yet I was warmed. The ice-field had slackened its grip and between the loose pans, mirrors of water reflected the light. Ice-sentinels, looking soft and inviting, waved at us, inviting us to come on.

Perry and Rodney came out with guns and ammo and a short while later a plume of black smoke engulfed me and the first shock of the day foundered thirty decapitated carcasses over me, surrounding me up to my waist. Startled back to reality, I stood up and watched the blood drip off my blubber clothes. "How much, in the name of God, is this worth an hour?"

Darrell and Paul came up the ladder sweating profusely, steaming around the head and neck. "Someone else stow the meat," Darrell said, pulling off his greasy rubber gloves and wiping his brow with his hand. "My back is just about gone."

"And mine's no better," Paul said, going directly to the rail, unclasping the buttons on his shining blubber clothes as he went. That meant Randy and me in the hold.

Reaching in over with my foot and placing it on the rung of the steep, steel ladder, I applied my weight. My boot slipped to the side and I almost fell down the hold. Gerard grabbed me, saving me by wrenching on my shoulder. I shrieked out in pain, fright and relief and got a hold on myself. "It's better to go down the ladder, Mick," he said, easing up his hold on me.

"Thanks, Gerard," I said, continuing my way down. Half-way down, the hull slammed to starboard, flinging me against the bulkhead, banging my shoulder, hip and knee simultaneously. I yelped in pain and held on while Gerard grabbed for things on the hatch. A hakipik fell, striking me on the shoulder when I ducked my head in reaction to my seeing it coming. The hull straightened on course and I tried to pull myself together, shaken, rattled and bruised.

All the boys could do as they looked down at me was to try to keep from laughing. The image of their good-natured faces collided with the reality of my physical pain. I looked up, shook my head, and started to laugh. "Timing is everything," I said, straightening out my hurt knee, resuming my trek below into the gloom and stench of the centre pound.

It was the opposite of glorious down here. I was in the centre pound standing atop a pile of bloody ice. The space, the shape of the hull, was divided into twelve pounds; four port side, four starboard and four up the centre.

The forward starboard pound was filled with pelts, the meat went port side aft. The bottom of this pound was covered with meat from the day before, up to a height of three pound-boards. Other greasy pound-boards filled the empty pounds along with rope, hooks, and water buckets. I shifted out as Randy scampered down the ladder.

"Stand back," he said, stepping in beside me. "The boys are going to throw some down. Put up your hood."

I got it up just after the first fifty pounds splattered in front of me in a spray of icy blood that struck me square in the face. I spun away spitting. A steady stream of grotesque bodies rained down for three minutes, spattering everything, Randy and me included. "Hold up!" he bellowed and the sickening rain stopped.

Wasting no time, he reached out and grabbed one in each hand and tossed it in the pound. I reached for one of the bloody things and it slithered out of my grasp. I grabbed again, this time driving my fingers into the knife wound between its ribs. I plucked too hard, the soft flesh ripped apart and I lost my grip on the slimy thing. Randy was tossing in his fourth before I got a firm hold with both hands, dragged it over myself and tossed it. It was very hot and I was sweating profusely and swearing incessantly by the time the meat needed icing.

Randy, with his head steaming, grabbed a shovel and stepped back into the pound. He shoveled the bloody ice up and spread it over the meat. It was hard, awkward work in the deepening confines. Once he had it liberally covered, he stepped in next to me. "Meat in the hold!" he shouted.

Down it rained and spattered again for a short flurry and we repeated the process adding boards as the pound filled, sweating, puffing and straining in the gore below decks. We each took a turn shovelling ice.

Sweat trickled down my back and chest, and dropped from my jaws just as the blood flowed freely down the sides of the hatch.

Randy's suit was crimson, his boots a dripping red. His face was awash with sweat mixed with blood and he grunted and groaned and strained and blasphemed the dirt of it all. The big dogs came down in four repulsive sixty-pound chunks and I had to literally cuddle them in my arms to get them stowed. To fill the extreme inside of the pound, we used a short gaff. I'd toss the cursed carcass atop the pile and Randy would drive in the hook and push it inside. Looking at him and working beside him, I knew exactly how he felt.

"Bloody stuff. It's not worth anything! If we get into the seals, we'll be dumping this over the sides," he said, when we sat back waiting for the shower of gore to stop. "Six dollars a carcass, that's what it's worth, but it pays some expenses. It's better than empty pounds."

"That's all there is and there ain't no more," the voice said from above. Darrell poked his head down in the hold, looked at me there huddled just like Randy. "I know that must break your heart."

Looking back at him, I sang, "Heart! Break my heart! My heart is broke. It's spread all over the sea. It's a sea of tears...a sea of heartbreak; lost love and loneliness, memories of your caress, so divine, how I wish...," I continued on to sing the verse.

Darrell laughed and shouted, "Sing it up!"

I sang another couple of verses and left it at that. That was all I could muster. We finished the job and came up. All the ice was gone from the centre pound.

The sun was above the cloak when I came up. It shone unobstructed from a clear, blue sky; the shroud of fog and frost hugged the floes. The pools of mirror-smooth water reflected the rays back into my face, causing me to sneeze three or four violent times.

"God bless you," Gerard said, sharpening up his knife.

"Thanks, Gerard," I replied, then two more sneezes racked my aching body. "I'd sooner be kicked in the testicles than have to sneeze!" I said, between the sniffs, snorts, snots and spits.

The ship slowed. Number one for the day was in range. *Bang! Bang!* Paul walked over and picking out his gaff said, "This puppy is mine."

"Be my guest."

He sat with one leg over the rail, waiting for the time to come. The smell of coffee drifted across my nose and my stomach rumbled to life. I caught the scent of toast and David stuck his head out the galley window, saying "Breakfast for two served in five minutes." Gerard elected me and Darrell saying, "We'll hold the fort."

"Have yourself a good hot breakfast," Paul said, springing from the rail. *Scrunch!* Gerard sprayed and Darrell scrubbed me through the perishing wash-cycle. I was surprised to find I didn't shiver my way through all of it. With the brush, most of the blood washed off me. "You're good enough," Gerard said, turning the hose on Darrell. I took the brush from him and returned the favour.

David was lying on the floor, pulling on Paul's survival suit when I went inside. "Skipper told me to go up in the spar," he said, without me asking. I helped him with the clasps and zippers. He didn't look to be in very good shape. I knew he was managing his own misery. "I don't envy you," I said. He rolled his eyes and gritted his teeth then reached for the frosty door handle.

Darrell was pouring hot tea into his mug by the time I got to the galley. The toaster popped four brown slices of bread. "I got ham put on for you," he said.

At that moment I felt hungry and comfortable and accepted gracefully. "Yes please and as long as you're at it, I'll have a few hot beans and two slices of toast to go along with it."

"Coming right up, sir," he responded. "Take a seat and I'll have that for you in a few minutes." He gestured me towards the table.

"You're most kind," I said with a bow, sitting down in the skipper's place.

As Darrell passed me a cup of hot tea, Perry came in holding his steamed up glasses in his hands. Ripping off a paper towel, he cleaned his lenses and came towards me. I shifted in. His face was leather brown and his teeth were drift-ice white.

"How are you feeling now?" he asked.

"Here and now skipper, I'm the best kind," I replied, squeezing the tea bag to the side of the mug. "But I can't say the same while

I'm on the open deck."

"Yes, it's cold isn't it, boy? Perishing. On the wheel-house, that's where it's cold! It must be twenty below and there's not a draft of wind."

"I believe you and you can take off another twenty degrees in the spar."

"It's going to be a nicer day later on. If the ice keeps going apart, we'll use the speedboat. I just hope there's a few seals."

The hot tea must have released something in me that prompted me to say, "Yes sir, now we're ready for four hundred."

"Yes, boy," he acknowledged, "It'd be all right. That's not much to ask for."

I didn't respond right away. I just sort of munched over the thought of asking for the horrors four hundred entailed. I munched away at my breakfast and as my stomach received the food, it did its mysteries again and I heard myself say, "There's thirteen million of them out here. When are we going to get into them?"

"From last reports, we're not that far from the herd, twelve to fifteen miles at the most. Later on today, if the ice goes abroad, we should be in some seals. There was five or six boats in the midst of them yesterday." Finishing his tea, he went into the wheel-house.

"Radio seals," Darrell remarked. "We need real seals."

The ship stopped and we heard the rifle's report. "There's one now."

"One at a time. Old man, at one-at-a-time, we'll need all of June to load this one."

Leaving my dirty dishes in the sink, I went to the forecastle for my sunglasses. I'd be needing them today. Out here glint turns to glare and I didn't want to suffer the misery of snow-blindness. It was all I could do to keep from crawling into my bunk. Instead I said goodbye to my pillow.

Things were slow on deck. Gerard was pelting a steaming, young, fat harp and Paul was using the axe on another. Blood streaked the deck. One lay bleeding beside the gunnels. Battling on my crispy, repulsive blubber clothes, I again resigned myself to the misery. Steeling my knife, I positioned him "belly-up" between my feet with my sigh turning to steam in front of my face. A burp escaped my mouth and the smell of beans and seal guts whisked up my nose. I hardly had him gutted when the rifle fired. Putting down my knife, I picked up the greasy gaff and took my position by the rail. Randy indicated port side with a wave of his arm. Rodney was in the control booth, David was high in the rigging, glowing orange against a clear, blue sky.

The ice surface was hard and slippery but I skipped, hopped and jumped my way up to the dead harp and returned without mishap. I hopped in over the rail feeling invigorated. The Hunt was on again.

Three jumps later we came in view of our first hoods, an old dog, a mature bitch and two fat, "blue-back" pups together on a pan. I watched as the old dog slipped into the slob, disappearing beneath the floes. Hoods are a different species from harps. They are larger, more aggressive and some males weigh in excess of one thousand pounds. One hundred yards from them, Rodney stopped the boat and the sharp report of the two high-powered rifles cracked the crispy air. That was my cue to go and I responded by flinging myself clear the railing, landed with a scrunch underfoot, ran, hopped, skipped and jumped towards the big, dead bitch and her dead twins quietly bleeding out beside her. Sprinting and jumping across the slob-filled cracks, I tried not to think about the monster that lurked somewhere beneath. I suppressed the memories of stories I'd heard about old dog hoods. "...no good to hit him on the head...only chance you got is to drive your gaff down his throat and run...if he gets a hold of you, if he pulls you in...." With a stomach full of fluttering butterflies, all pissing adrenaline, I made my way up to the blood pan, knelt beside them and waited for the old dog to show.

She was a lot larger than any dog harp we had killed, and she lay perfectly still, quietly spurting a fountain of hot blood. Crouching beside her, I didn't feel very big. The *C. Michelle* rolled slowly in the swells, Perry looking down the barrel of the rifle. Randy watched beside him while Rodney watched from the control booth. The pans gnawed and ate each other as they shifted about with the tide and swells. The closest slob was ten feet away. I waited for him to show, hoping he wouldn't surface so as to put me in the line of fire. I readied my gaff and braced myself to run somewhere.

I tried to suppress the thoughts of a scene from last year's Hunt when an old bitch hood lay on the pan with her pups. The dog bobbed in the water close by. Perry shot his family and I waited beside them for fifteen minutes before Perry ordered them taken aboard and we proceeded on. As I sat on the stern, looking at the blood pan fall away in the wake, the giant charged out of the water and in an instant was sniffing and smelling the area where his mate and family had been. He reared his head, swelling his hood into a balloon of fury, and looking directly at me, he launched from the pan and crashed into the frigid water. I watched the wake for him to show.

I was jolted back to reality by a great gush of air when the old dog reared his great head, twenty yards away from me. He was blowing the loose skin atop his head into a tight balloon of flesh when a bullet exploded in his brain and the beast slipped back into the slob.

At the sound, I charged forward towards him, skipping the pans on the run. Seeing the bloodstain, I drove my gaff in, hooking him just below the surface. Taking the strain, I pulled the head of this gigantic ice-monster up on the pan.

"Good job!" the skipper called from the bridge. The long-liner surged forward in a puff of smoke. Almost abreast of us, the ship stopped and Darrell ran up to me with his gaff and together we pulled the great beast out of the water. The winch screeched when he went in over the rail.

Back aboard, using a meat hook, I helped Darrell roll him over on his back. He placed the blade of his knife below the lower lip and applied pressure. The fur split abroad, exposing three inches of blubber the full length of his ten-foot body. Small geysers of blood spurted along the massive ribcage, spraying Darrell's face before he could pull away. Pulling back and raising his arm to shield himself, he thrust his blade into the exposed chest. Viciously, he ripped upwards, severing at least four ribs. Blood gushed from the wound and spilled onto the deck. Pulling away to escape it, we stood back and waited for it to bleed out. "How many gallons of blood do you think is in him?" I asked.

"Must be twenty gallons at least. He's been bleeding for ten minutes and it's still gushing out. Yes sir, it's no harm to call them bloody things."

Straddling the great specimen, I chopped open the ribcage with the axe. Exposing the entrails, we were shrouded in a cloud of pungent steam. I held the ribcage open with the meat hook to help Darrell extricate the massive innards. "It's the same thing as paunching a bull moose," he said, holding the steaming conglomerate up by the dripping heart, that I guessed, weighed twelve solid pounds. Three small turbot oozed out of his ruptured stomach.

"There's his breakfast," I said, indicating the turbot.

Darrell grabbed up the fish and shouted up to the top deck, "Skipper, look what we found in this one. You tell me now, they don't eat fish!"

Perry came back to the railing, and looked at the fish in his hands, saying, "There you go now. Show that to IFAW." We hung the seal from the boom and measured him; ten feet two inches; the depth sounder showed 130 fathoms.

I used the hook to pull over the massive carcass to make Darrell's work easier. I moved the sharp tip just as he moved his hand; the hull lurched. The hook pierced the side of his rubber glove and stapled his hand solidly to the meat. He looked directly at me and calmly said, "Not that meat, Mick."

Very much relieved that I had missed his hand, I unstapled him. "Man, that was close!"

Putting the dripping gloves up in front of my face, he said, "That's a new pair of gloves you owe me."

"That's a small price that I'll gladly pay," I replied, resuming the gory chore. A few minutes later, the giant was washed, pelted, quartered and cooling on the stern. That four hundred pounds of meat brought six dollars. The ten inch penis brought eighty. We turned toward the bitch. "If you shoot a bitch…."

At 9:00 A.M. the day was brightening up. Looking directly into the glare, I could feel the heat of the sun on my face. It was going to be a good day for hunting. The wind was but a breeze and the tide was ripping up the ice-field. The fog was gone and the three-metre swells kept everything in motion. We were making good time, weaving through loose ice into open leads of water.

Bang! Bang! Bang! Bang! Bang! The smell of gunpowder drifted up my nostrils just before the smoke from the stack covered me and the hull lurched forward. I knew by the report that they were "small ones" and looking into the rigging, I saw David hold up three fingers, indicating starboard side. "Over the side, Mickey." I picked a gaff and got ready.

By 11:00 A.M., we had thirty cooling, six of them old hoods. Perry stopped the boat and ordered the speedboat readied, armed, launched and manned. Paul and Randy were on their way into the floes in less than fifteen minutes. That left Darrell, Gerard and myself. Darrell and I took turns jumping. Gerard was always there to accept the gaff and pluck the seal in over the rail. Not always did this happen cleanly and often, due to poor footing or open water around the hull, the "toss-pull" technique often fell short and all the exertion was wasted when the seal bounced off the rail and fell back into the sea. This was very hard, taxing work.

At 4:00 P.M. we saw the speedboat working its way toward us and we stopped in a small lake. Watching them zig-zag through the loose ice, I had an urge to get off the ship. By the time the thirty-five seals were unloaded, I really wanted to go. I jumped aboard and bailed out the gallons of blood while Paul and Randy got a cup of tea and a lunch.

I used a plastic gallon container and the first ten scoops overflowed and sloshed around as I emptied it over the gunnel. The fiberglass-coated wooden speedboat was sixteen feet long, five feet wide; the outside hull was painted blue, the inside was supposed to be white. The *Blue Dolphin* was divided into four compartments by three tots. A gaff, a hakipik and a long hook lay across them. A life-jacket was secured to the plywood cuddy and my rifle was strapped to the rack; a kit bag was tucked in underneath. The floor was littered with spent .22 bullet casings. The blood made a large red cloud in the calm water and, finishing up, I thought of "Jaws." Sharks did frequent this area. I had often heard reports of sharks attacking the sculps left soaking in the sea overnight: pelts half eaten, ropes severed, money lost.

"Pass up the gas cans," Paul said.

Passing them up to him, I looked up at Perry and said, "I want a trip off in the speedboat."

"What?"

"I want a trip out in the speedboat. It's my rifle, I'd like to go with my rifle this time."

"Proper thing, Mickey boy. Take a trip out among the floes. It'll do you good," Paul said.

Randy stood in the stern by the engine, straightening things away. "I guess I got to break in a new man," he said, in a disgruntled-sounding voice.

"Break in a new man!" I echoed, "Buddy, I'll have you know I'm not a new man at this. What do you think I got that rifle for, shooting rats?"

He didn't reply, he didn't even turn towards me. I looked up at the skipper and said, "What about it?"

"Well boy, if you thinks you can do it, go ahead."

Three minutes later, we were speeding away from the long-liner, weaving our way through the loose pans. The wind buffeted me all the while it took to ready the gun. Then, holding the painter, I stood up on the tot to get a better view.

The tot was very slippery under my bloody boots and I had to fight for balance. The wind pressed my cold clothes to my body and brought water from my eyes. Squeezing my muscles together, I turned left and right scanning for seals. For some reason Randy slacked the throttle and I found myself going forward over the bow, the painter slack in my hand. To keep from going overboard, I stepped down quickly off the tot and sprawled forward across the life jacket.

I kept myself aboard at the expense of my knees, which banged against the plyboard edge, and my tender elbows, that smashed against the gunnel. Randy sped up the engine again. I turned my head to look at him and couldn't catch his eye. Saying nothing, I stepped upon the greasy tot again and, grasping the bowline, turned to scan the floes.

Wham! The bow struck an ice clump, causing me to have to quickly step down again, this time striking my other elbow and banging my knee. I turned to glare back at Randy but before I could start to chew him out, he pointed off to the starboard and said, "Seal over there."

Turning around, my eyes immediately picked up the "black on white," lying three hundred yards across the ice-speckled swells. Sitting on the tot, I unstrapped the rifle and placed the stock upon the lifejacket. In order to focus the cross-hairs on the target, I had to slump down and press my ribs firmly against the gunnel and twist my right knee in an awkward angle across the tot. Placing my left hand atop the scope, I focused on the sleeping young harp. Huddling in the cuddy, I got ready for the shot.

WHAM! A pan struck the bow next to my ribs, tossing me across the tiny space. I held on to the rifle and absorbed the impact, being extremely careful not to strike the scope. The shock knocked the wind out of me and I gasped in air. Recovering, I scrambled back into firing position. Back on course, we closed on the target.

It's not an easy task to place a small bullet in the brain of a seal from an open boat. The slightest movement, the least contact with a pan, the rising and falling make it very difficult. At a hundred yards, I got ready and tried to focus on the skull. The seal lifted its head, came out of his sleep and stirred awake. Its head was partially hidden from view, and I waited for the right moment. "Give it to him!" Randy said, in a hushed, urgent voice, behind.

Not really wanting to, I squeezed the trigger and the piece exploded in the startled, young beater's face. Reloading, I spied it again, prancing away from me. "Shoot, Mick, shoot!" Randy repeated, excitedly from behind.

Turning away from the scurrying seal, I faced him and said,

"Randy, when I get the cross-hairs on their skulls, I'll waste no time dispatching them! Until then keep quiet and don't rock the boat."

"The seal is still there," he said.

Turning again, I focused on the beater. It made the "stop-for-a-last-look-at-the-edge-of-the-pan" mistake and I sighted its watery eyes looking directly at me. Squeezing the trigger, a puff of smoke and fur shot from its head and it dropped to the pan. Putting the rifle in the rack, I prepared to bring it aboard.

Randy drove the boat into the pan and I jumped out. Cutting the engine hard over, he slewed the pan while I ran for the harp. I was glad to see the blood spurting from its skull. When I grabbed the rear flippers, it slipped out of my grasp. Pulling off my gloves and putting them inside my coat, I bent again and grabbed it. The fur was soft and warm. The seal was at least eighty pounds and I dragged it, leaving a trail of crimson to the speedboat. There, I lifted and tossed it in the centre section, directly in front of Randy. It landed with a spray of hot blood. Number one was aboard. Pushing off the boat, I boarded, placing my boots upon the gunnel, bracing myself for a slip. *Vroom!* Randy resumed our search and destroy mission. "Good shot," he said.

I stood atop the tot to scan. The exertion and thrill of the Hunt invigorated me, a sense of exhilaration whelmed up inside me. The wind whisked freshly by me, shooting inside my clothing. We skimmed our way through the dispersing ice-field in search of our quarry. Take no prisoners! Shoot to kill!

I saw another off to port and stepped down to get the rifle ready. Ejecting the spent cartridge, I pushed in a fresh round. Waiting for the distance to close, I watched the sleeping harp. The bed on which he slept was two feet above water. When we were within thirty yards of him, he was still sleeping peacefully on his side, stretched out, soaking up the evening, contentedly digesting our fish. At twenty yards I put down the gun and grabbed the hakipik. "I'll bat him."

Randy nodded in agreement and we quietly coasted up. The scrunching sound of my boots striking the pan and the jolt from the stem woke him up. He spied me and reared his head, displaying his sharp teeth in a defiant gesture. The only defence the pups have is to pull their heads back into their shoulders. No defence against a hakipik. I brought it viciously down upon his scull seeing my reflection in his eyes which stayed wide open until the iron head drove his skull to the ice. The limp body immediately relaxed, the head slowly stretching out from between the shoulders. Again and again in rapid succession I brought down the hakipik on the now pulverised skull, assuring myself he was dead. Claiming him, I dragged the squirming seal back to the waiting speedboat. Often, to save time, I'd sprint fifty yards across the floes to drag back the tow instead of taking the time to batter our way through. I knew just one slip and I'd never be seen or heard from again. No way was Randy going to get to me in seven seconds.

"That's the way to get them," Randy commented, after I tossed it in beside the first one.

"Yes," I said, jumping aboard, "it cuts down on overhead."

We both chuckled. *Vroom!* We picked up speed, resuming our general course, zig-zagging through the floes, about a mile from the *C. Michelle*. I could see her working to the west. Smoke billowed from the stacks, tainting the blue sky. From here she looked more like a toy than a ship. Muffled rifle reports sounded intermittently on the chilly wind.

At 5:30 P.M. Randy and I were cruising through loose ice, the evening brilliant with sunlight, the sea mirror-calm. Conditions were perfect for hunting but they were scarce. It gets cold quickly when seals are scarce and we only had fifteen aboard after searching thirty miles. Cruising up a long finger of water pointing into the heart of the pack, I spotted the black head in the water. "In the water," I said, pointing with my frozen hand. Randy spotted it immediately and steered towards it.

I slipped into the awkward firing position and sighted on him. Steadily we closed the distance as he bobbed and turned, playing "peek-a-boo" behind a small pan. One hundred yards from him, I focused him through the scope. His eyes sparkled where the cross hairs met and I fired. The distinct sound of bullet exploding in bone came to my ears, a puff of hair and blood shot from his head and he keeled over in the water. "Good shot!" Randy said.

"Thank you," I said, "and you did a fine job with the boat." As I kept my eyes on the floating harp, Randy brought us up alongside and pulled him aboard while I reloaded.

"I'm not going back until dark," he said, shutting off the engine and sitting down on the tot. "How many do we have?"

The centre pound was almost full. To get an accurate count, I shifted some of them into the next pound. "Twenty-four there."

"Where's the boat now?"

Standing on the tot, I spotted the smudge about two miles to the southwest, working the loose ice. "Over there."

"We'll work our way back and pick up a few more. That will burn up the rest of the evening. Pass me back the kit bag. Do you want a can of drink?"

We spent the next ten minutes eating his lunch of wieners and Coke, sitting in the speedboat, in the arctic icepack, ninety miles from the nearest land. The sea was serene, the environment friendly and peaceful, as nice as it gets out there. The sun was losing its power and the cold meat and fluids in my stomach sent a chill through me. "Would you sooner be on the boat or out here?" Randy asked.

Tossing my garbage in the bag, I answered, "I'd sooner be home. This is nice when the weather is nice and seals are plentiful but the accommodations stink."

"You're a good shot. Just as good as Paul, even better. If you want to, I'll mention it to Perry and you can come out whenever I go."

"It's good to get away from the boat. I like working with you and I feel that if worst came to worst, we'd survive out here for a couple of days. Sure, speak to Perry.

It was chilly speeding into the wind, standing on a tot in the front of the small boat watching uninhabited floes pass. I compressed all my muscles and hunched up against the piercing chill that attacked me through my zipperless coat. We killed just enough to keep my blood from freezing. The sky clouded over and most of the seals deserted to spend the night fishing. We shot a couple more in the water. Lights shone like a Christmas tree from the dragger as we approached it at dusk.

We unloaded thirty harps. The deck was clean of all other seals and over one hundred pelts were piled at the stern, like yaffles of split cod. A pile of meat steamed in the corner. By the time we had them sculped and washed, shifted and stowed, the speedboat loaded and readied, the deck and ourselves scrubbed clean, it was 10:30 P.M.

We finished the day with a disappointing 168 harps. Not good. We were two short of breaking even. Actually, we were still far from breaking even. These seals were only at the cooling stage. They had to be handled another six times minimum, for us to have "admission paid."

"We can't kill none 'till we find 'em," Paul said disappointedly. It had been one of those "nice" days at the ice when we should have killed four hundred.

Our foes lay peacefully about like sleeping menaces. Rodney and Paul lassoed a large one with the bowline and, beneath the lights in the spar, we finished the day. The air got crisper; it was going to get colder.

Radio seals filled all frequencies. "...six hundred, eight hundred, five and six on a pan...seals everywhere...." Perry added our pathetic few. It was no consolation to hear reports lesser than ours. One at a time we climbed into our bunks.

"Security. Security. Security. All stations, all stations...marine weather forecast issued for Monday, April 14th...Funk Island Bank...gale force easterlies, forty, gusting to fifty-five knots...."

"Another rotten day tomorrow," Gerard said from his bunk where he was reading a book. "We can't get a spell of good weather, can we?"

"Back to the misery again tomorrow," I said, shucking my clothes, groaning when the cloth came in contact with my sore muscles and bruised skin.

"You got a couple good bruises there," Randy said.

"Yes sir, you got that right," I assured him. "Trophies of the day.

You could even say I passed the day with shining colours; mostly black, blue, and red." I climbed painfully into my tomb. Finding enough comfort in my sleeping bag to quell my aches and pains, I succumbed into delirium, rocked in the cradle atop the "aquarium" seeing, when I closed my eyes, furry faces with watery eyes looming in my riflescope. Death knocked to get in.

Monday, April 14

My repose was shattered a short while later when the hull lurched violently and the tiny room filled with a crunching sound. The sea before the storm. "Gerard, take in the bow line, we got to move out of this! We'll be beat to pieces here," I heard Perry say, as the sea hurled the roped pan at us again.

Gerard scampered out of his bunk, hastily dressed and scurried up the ladder. I followed suit and was climbing the ladder when the Volvo roared to life. Pulling on my sweater, I followed Gerard through the open wheel-house door, onto the forward deck.

As I cleared the lee of the superstructure, the wind and driving sleet, hailed by forty-knot winds, brought me up standing and pushed me back a step. I gasped when the wind shot through me. Gritting my teeth and sucking in some frosty air, I braced myself and plunged ahead across the heaving bow towards Gerard, wrestling with an ice-covered knot.

The engine roared and the hull lurched when Perry gave her throttle ahead to provide slack for us. I pushed off and stumbled towards him just as the bow struck the heaving icesheet. I staggered over Gerard's shoulders and fell in a pile against the ice-crusted gunnel, absorbing the shock with my sore shoulder. Forgetting the stabbing pain, I lunged forward, grabbed the nylon rope, and pulled in some slack for him. Two hull-shuddering blows later we were pulling in the fifty fathoms of rope.

Freed from the pan, Perry turned hard to starboard and gave her throttle to clear the immense, tossing sheet. The hundred-ton piece slammed into the bow when we veered away into the darkness, the driving rain shooting like arrows in the beam of the searchlight.

The impact and subsequent lurch tossed us both against the gunnels with a thud. Gerard couldn't help but fall on me and I had his weight added to the crunching my body received. Before the pressure released, and the hull straightened on course, I'm sure I had felt three ribs crack. The air shot from my lungs. The numbness of the snarling, piercing wind, the freezing, stinging ice pellets and the fact that we had another twenty fathoms of rope over the rail inspired me to push Gerard back up off me and we both regained control. A few bone rattling seconds later, the end of the rope flicked in through the rausechauk. Turning, I very thankfully went back inside, frozen to the very core. I was wet and wide-awake. It had taken four minutes. I shivered myself warm in the wheel-house watching Perry navigate our way through the violent seas, most times zig-zagging clear of the most monstrous menaces.

Gerard came in off deck. Water soaked his beet-red face. I knew it wasn't sweat. He shook uncontrollably. "It's not nice out there," he said.

"Not fit for anything!" Perry snarled, working the controls. "You know it's not fit!" He braced himself as the sea hurled another hundred tons at us, the shock shivering the lurching hull from stem to stern, mast to keel. Charts fell to the floor, pots and pans clanged in the galley, the prop chewed ice.

Darrell's head poked up from the forecastle as we lurched our way through the violence. He said nothing. Looking through the wind-lashed, sleet-spattered windows at a search light beam filled with arrows, he held on and absorbed the shocks and tremors as they came, like the rest of us.

It was 2:30 A.M. and come they did, relentlessly and violently, all night long. It felt like we were in a never-ending demolition derby. No one spoke much while the long-liner rolled and careened with the powerful punches. The pelts in the hold and on deck added to the bulk and the ship struck solidly time and time and time again.

"What a night to abandon ship," I thought.

It was no good to lie down, but eventually I had to. It basically came down to where you preferred to be beaten to pieces, so I chose my bunk. Climbing in between the collisions, I covered up to the chin. I couldn't get warm; my core wouldn't thaw. "What a day to have to work," I thought, my mind plunging into the depths of despair in unison with the plunges of the hull, the only difference being that my spirit failed to rise.

The elements confirmed my dire straits with a solid smash to the hull, next to my ear. I rubbed across the foam mattress, striking my sore knee back to life. "Two hundred today and I'll have earned about sixty dollars." The thought of two hundred on a day like this irked me. I shivered in the fetal position, wondering where the next one was going to strike, not caring if it came right alongside me.

It didn't let up and we couldn't give up. We had to punch it out holding our own throughout the turbulent hours of impenetrable darkness, filled to bursting with anxious moments. By daylight, the collisions were less frequent but each and every consecutive one displayed the unleashed power of the sea. The increasing visibility gave us back the advantage of sight, making navigation a great deal less hazardous. Thrown around in my bunk, I knew, by the roll of the hull and the pitch of the wind outside, exactly what I'd see out there: wind and rain, slop-snow and stinging ice pellets, millions upon millions of them, cold and hard; ocean swells awesomely lifting, to a height of twelve feet, hundreds of millions of tons of solid ice, all around me. I wasn't ready to see that yet.

Add to that the fat, the blood, the slipping and sliding, the sweating and straining, the cooling and heating. I swallowed a lump of something that stuck to the back of my dry throat, groaned, held on and absorbed the punches. Never again!

I was beaten out of bunk at 8:00 A.M. to exactly what I expected. Looking at the snow accumulated halfway up the windows, I knew I didn't have to look any further. I shook my head in heavy-hearted disgust and submissive resignation. I was knocked and shaken, thrown and tossed around, all through my breakfast of cereal, juice, toast and tea. It was all I could do to keep the dishes on the table. No one was too well pleased.

The galley got stuffy while we punched the time. Paul reached behind Randy's back to open the window. Raw winds and icy sleet attacked the back of his neck. Randy sprang clear of the draft, looked at Paul and said, "Close that up, boy, before we perish!"

Paul took the time to look directly into the onslaught and said in a disgusted tone of voice, "Wouldn't that just turn your guts. Everything is coated with glitter."

"Not only turn them, you're freezing mine," Randy responded, reaching back and sliding the glass closed. Paul shook his head and stared at the icy water, streaming across the steamed up window.

At 9:00 A.M. Gerard said the dreaded words no one wanted to hear but all knew were coming, "Let's stow down the fat."

"You're a slave-driver, Gerard," I said, drinking down my last sips of tea, thinking of the 168 pelts and carcasses: greasy, cold, bloody, heavy, slippery...The heat, the cold, the wind, the rain, the sleet, the hours...Reluctantly, I resigned myself to the miseries and pushed up from the table. Everyone was filing out.

It was harsher than I expected on deck, more barbaric. The wind squalled and rampaged all around me. The black smoke barely escaped the stack before it was gobbled up by the gale. Add to that the glitter. Everything was coated with it; the deck, the gunnels, the speedboat, the pelts, the meat, everything shone with ice. Gerard and Paul were breaking a path across the deck using wooden mallets.

"Give me a hand to lift off this cover, Mick," Darrell said, grabbing hold of the hatch-cover and shaking the glistening ice loose.

Cautiously shifting around him, I reached in over to lift the heavy, slippery cover. *Wham!* I registered a blow to my kidneys as though someone had sneaked up behind me and punched me. Wheeling around, I expected to see someone's face, into which I was going to drive my fist at full force. No one was there. My eyes caught sight of a chunk of ice, the size of a baseball, skidding across the deck. Glitter from the rigging.

Perry came out the door wearing rubber clothes over his insulated suit, a fur hat on his head and holding a rifle in his hands. Over his shoulder hung the ammo tin and around his neck dangled binoculars. "Boys, come over and clear the ice from the ladder and the top deck," he said. "It's slippery enough to break my neck up there this morning."

Gerard and Paul shifted their efforts. There was ice all around: ice on my clothes, ice in the wind, ice on the sea, ice in my veins, ice, ice, ice.

Darrell shovelled up the shattered sleet and tossed it down the hold. "We need ice," he said.

I stood for a minute allowing my mind to express itself. "Man, this is barbaric! It's not fit to be out. No way should a man have to work in these miserable conditions. It's not sensible! I wouldn't put a Siberian husky outside on a day like this!" Things tossed, rolled, swung and swayed, nothing stood still. Off clear the deck, everything rose and fell, drifted and swirled. The rain made everything glisten.

Barbaric! Sealers were barbarians. It was true. You had to be a barbarian to stand it. Everything else was barbaric: the wind, the sea, the sky, the lurching ice fields, the elements, the environment, everything! If you didn't become barbaric, you didn't last.

A piece of ice exploded beside me and I braced myself instinctively. Darrell reached down to pick up the carcasses scattered from the pile, tossing them down the hold. He then reached for the pelts. I followed suit. Making my first trek across the rolling deck to retrieve my lift, I wasn't feeling very good. The top tier was glazed over and I shattered it with the heel of my boot. When I plunged my hand in the flipper hole, it felt greasy, heavy and repulsively cold, exactly as expected. Bearing their weight, I dragged them back and, lifting them over the lip, dropped them down. The greasy deck was treacherous and I slipped down twice. Ice bombs burst all around me; some were direct hits.

Paul and Gerard finished clearing the top deck. Darrell and Paul escaped to the hold, Randy and Gerard joined in dragging the pelts. One lurch brought Randy off his feet in an instant, but he was lucky enough to fall on top.

Once, at maybe trek fifty, I was robotically going back and forth and suddenly I recalled a nature program I had seen on TV about Emperor Penguins in Antarctica. They walked in circles to keep warm on the glaciers. I could relate to those on the outside of the circle.

The supply ran out a desolate while later, and before the meat could be stowed, we needed ice. Rodney pulled up beside a high clumpered pan, Paul and I jumped out with axes. It was scary. I did most of my chopping from a kneeling position because each time I stood, the rocking action of the pan had a tendency to toss me into the slobby water. The violent action caused me to miss my aim with the axe and I struck the wooden handle across the hard edge, snapping it in two. The steel head glanced off the flint-hard sheet, whizzed along by Paul's knee disappearing with a splash in the slob. Throwing the handle part I held in my hand at the splash, I turned to look at Perry whose head was poking over the rail. Shrugging my shoulders, I said, "Now we have one net-bag and one axe."

He was shaking his head when I turned back to the task at hand. I held open the net-bag and Randy tossed in the chunks Paul had chopped off. The hull drifted, despite Rodney's best efforts, and each time he brought the lurching hull in contact with the edge, the air exploded with the sound of scrunching ice; a sound that made me think of the effect that scrunch would have on my body. The winds lashed me without mercy, the rain stung me with fury and the pan tried to toss me. It wasn't a very good location.

"Yes sir, yes sir, three bags full" and we gathered together to get aboard. The hull crunched the edge while we waited for our timing. Paul and Randy scampered aboard leaving me alone.

The force of the impact veered the hull away and out of my reach. Rodney fought for control. I climbed higher atop another frozen chunk and waited my chance. With the wind lashing me and water blurring my vision, I watched the heaving hull come nearer. It was almost within reach when the sheet beneath my feet collapsed and I dropped down. Thinking I was going into the sea, I braced myself for the shock and looked toward the boat. An eternal, heart-swallowing instant later, the sheet settled onto a pan below, stopping my fall. With great relief, I saw the rail and scampered in over, white as a sheet.

"What a fright I got then!" I said to Gerard after I'd regained my composure. "I thought I was in the water."

"You should have seen the look on your face," he said with a grin. "Too bad I didn't get you on video."

"Gerard, if my insurance agent ever saw a video of that, he'd cut me off quicker than you can pelt a young harp," I replied, with true conviction. He laughed a little longer.

I watched the pan fall away astern, quickly gobbled up by the storm. The spaces of open water were lathered in froth and the white-capped waves atop the four-metre swells reminded again me of grinding teeth.

"That axe hasn't hit bottom yet," Gerard said, waving the other at me. The thought made me shiver again while I shovelled the pieces of ice into the centre pound after he busted the chunks up with the back of the axe. Paul took a spell at it and Darrell finished them off. When the last of it was shovelled down, I went to the ladder and backed cautiously into the hold. Randy joined me.

Work conditions were no different: dripping sweat and revolting blood, grease, grunts, and curses. We toiled for an hour before the last one was chinked into place with the gaff and iced. Three of the twelve pounds were filled. I followed Randy up the ladder for wash-down and breakfast. The thought of hot tea and something to eat was suddenly very appealing.

An hour later, I was back huddled by the hydraulic lines, the same as if I had never left. My stomach was fuller and the hot food and tea thawed my core a little, but other than that, things were the same: rain, sleet, wind and hundreds of tons of ice, slowly rising up and down.

We'd mill together for a spell, then we'd split abroad about the deck, each enduring his own misery in his own way. It was stressful enough not to be killing seals. We were two short of being almost even; almost having paid the admission fee that privileged us to be on the cutting edge of the once "Greatest Hunt in the World."

"Greatest for whom?" I wondered, clutching the "life-supporting" hot pipes. The merchants, the plant owners and ship owners took the lion's share; the sealers took the most chances with life and limb, did all the dirty work, endured the greatest hardships, suffered the greatest pains, and paid the greatest prices before receiving their meagre share. Where "glory" was involved, the sealers received none of that. The great captains kept that for themselves. It was always "the seals I got," not "the jumps they made and the chances they took."

Gerard broke my train of thought by saying, "Chin up, my friend. This will all be over in another ten days."

"Come on, dark!" was the only reply I could think of.

Bang! Bang! Bang! Perry had a big one killed, port side. "Over the side, Mickey."

I saw it through the sleet, coming around the hull on a single rocking pan. It was a big old dog hood. Gerard operated the winch controls and slackened the boom line as I grabbed the hook. I knew the procedure: jump out with the hook, toss the rope over his head, pull it back under his chest and shoulders, hook the rope, pull tight, and let the winch pull him aboard. I had done it many times before.

My blubber clothes cracked and resisted when I forced them to comply, reflecting how I felt inside. I saw my chance and jumped with the rope and hook in my hands.

Landing safely, I ran up to the eight hundred-pound fish-eater and straddled his large back with my feet. Bending over him, I started to pull the rope under his head. He sprayed a geyser of blood, a foot into the air. I was about to straighten up to finish the chore, when he reared up and struck me in the chest with the side of his monstrous head. The force from the blow drove me off him and I found myself eight feet away, sprawled on the broad of my back, dripping and covered in hot, steaming blood.

Frozen with fright, I saw the beast rear again and attempt to turn in my direction. My greasy boots slipped on the ice, preventing me from scurrying away. Perry fired again and his head dropped to the pan. The force of the impact caused a wave-like ripple through him that was absorbed by the fat on his neck. He didn't move.

I didn't feel like moving either. "Go get him, Mick!"

I approached him again, striking him two or three vicious times on the skull with the hook before cautiously pulling the rope under him for the second time, ready for him to rear at any instant. He remained perfectly still this time and I held the rope tight until the winch screeched him aboard.

He was a big one and he steamed and bloodied the deck. From his stomach spilled two seal flippers. "They even eat their own," I said. Pulling his mouth open with the gaff, I was not surprised to find that my thigh could easily fit between his long, sharp teeth. I shivered though I wasn't cold.

"How would you like that to grab you?" Gerard said, breaking abroad the split pelvic bone with the heel of his boot. Ice crashed down haphazardly around us. There was nothing we could do about it.

"He almost did," I replied.

"That's right, so he did. Well, he won't be grabbing anything else," he added, holding the fifty pounds of steaming, dripping organs in his arms for all to see, before tossing them over the rail. Ten minutes later the great hood was pelted, quartered, washed, stowed and steaming on the stern. Number one for the day at 10:00 A.M.

Two families of hoods lying dead ahead broke the monotony of the day. Crashing up to the first family, Perry quickly and efficiently took out the mother and her two pups. I waited nervously beside them for ten minutes before I was called aboard, leaving the slaughtered family quietly bloodying up the pan. The old dog reared frighteningly close a couple of heart-stopping times but Perry couldn't get a shot.

Back aboard. Rodney rushed on the next family one thousand yards ahead. This old dog died beside his family and in jig time we had them aboard. As the ship turned back toward the dead hoods left on the pan, I watched from the top deck to see the elusive old dog, in an instant, surge out of the water up beside his dead mate.

Blowing the loose skin atop his massive head bullet-proof tight, he waddled up to and mounted the passive dead bitch. Oblivious to our approach he played out the reproduction act, making the "beast with two backs." Perry lodged a .243 bullet in his brain. Shaking his monstrous head, his body continuing the motions, he sprayed bone, brains and blood for twenty yards before collapsing atop his receptive mate.

"What a way to go!" I exclaimed turning for the aft deck to jump out and bring them aboard.

Rushing up to them with the tow hook, we noticed that even though the beast was dead as a nit, his body still pumped up and down. Putting the rope around his immense bulk a minute later, I feared he'd come awake. He didn't. I hooked the hook and gave the signal. Gerard engaged the winch. The rope tightened and above the noise of grinding ice, a few decibels higher than the purr of the Volvo, we all heard the long, loud "*slurrpppp!*" Darrell was first to laugh out loud and bellow, "That's a one-hundred-dollar slurp if I ever heard one." We all burst out laughing.

As we cleaned them up, sculping one large seal each, the deck became covered in steam and blood. In spite of it all we managed a few lewd comments and a few chuckles. After that fray, I spent most of the hideous day retrieving just enough seals, young and old, to keep *rigor mortis* from setting in.

6:00 P.M. found us in tighter ice, the herd eluding us in the relentless rain and wind. Twisting, turning, and careening our way at high RPMs through the floes, we encountered an immense field of tight ice, several square miles in area. Lying about, showing up like black specks, was a herd of old harps. Rodney stuck the bow of the long-liner in and we stopped.

"Fine lot of seals ahead," Perry said. "Great chance to make up a day's pay."

The herd, numbering in the hundreds of thousands, spread over two square miles. They watched our approach and some were wary enough to scurry. We stopped within range of two hundred. Perry and Randy opened up on them, firing at will, in rapid succession.

Watching, I saw the seals come alive and die. Some scurried off without hesitation. The great dogs were easy to spot, their black saddles standing out in the gloom. Some of them died at the edge of the pan, some of them died where they were. Some were destined to die later as a few of those struck down found life enough in their fatally wounded bodies to slide into the slob. Spent gunpowder swirled in the wind, heads dropped, seals fled, spent bullet casings tingled on deck. After two minutes, the floes within three hundred yards were deserted, except for the dead. Within an hour we had twenty-eight heaped in a bleeding pile and the long-liner made its way deeper into the midst of the small herd.

Darrell climbed atop the pile of harps to retrieve the steel chokers. I heard him yell and pluck back his foot, then fall across the heap. He pulled his leg up to his chest and amid all the noise, I heard the rip. Rolling off the pile, he stood up and, lifting his knee, showed us the legs of his blubber pants. A large piece was cleanly bitten out and the seam was ripped to well above his knee.

"Look at that!' he exclaimed. "That wouldn't turn your guts now. A brand new pair of rubber pants spoiled. Sixty bucks gone just as quick as that! Son of a bitch! I'll kill it! I'll kill it!"

I stood back and watched while he attacked the pile. Grabbing the dead seals by the rear flippers, he threw them about, not looking nor caring where they landed. Deeper he dug into the foundering heap, uttering, "Where are you, you bloody thing!"

Spotting him, he pulled away three more corpses to expose the bit of life. I saw that life in the eyes of one with rubber cloth between his teeth. His face was a muck of blood. "There you are," I heard Darrell say, reaching for the hakipik. "Well I got something for you!"

With that he brought the hakipik down in a deadly blow, striking the harp on the top of the skull. "How's that for starters!" he fumed, raising it over his head and striking the skull again. The leg of his ripped pants flapped in the wind as he brought down a third vicious blow. "Son of a bitch!"

Sweating and breathing hard, he threw the hakipik down. The old dog's head was pulverized; one eye hung from its socket, the other stared grotesquely at me. A piece of green rubber still hung from its mouth. The boat stopped again; seals lay all about, looking inquisitively at us. I knew what was coming. They did not.

Twice more before dark we made a slaughter, and at dusk the pans were deserted. David had fish cooking. The fragrant aroma swirled on the biting wind, sending a pang of hunger deep into my shrunken stomach. Seals were scattered about the deck, taking up almost all the space. Under the glare of the floodlights, we made room to wash down and strip off our blubber clothes in preparation for supper.

Wallowing in the slow swells, nudged by the ice, we all ate together. David placed a steaming pot of codfish, a large bowl of steaming hot potatoes, a dipper of fried fat pork and onions and a dish of creamy "drawn butter" on the table. After the blessing and the flurry of reaching, passing, "excuse mes" and "thank yous," we dug in to eat.

"Where are you getting your fish?" I asked David, liberally spooning grease over a chunk of boiled cod.

"Co-op," he replied, waiting for me to finish with the grease. "We paid fifteen dollars for that bit of fish."

"It'll never go up to what it's worth," I replied, lifting a flaky forkful to my mouth, savouring the exquisite taste.

"Just imagine," Randy said, "We're fishermen, making our living on the sea and we got to pay through the teeth for a little bit of fish."

"The seals will eat it anyway," Gerard put in. "How much fish do you think the herd we just hunted is going to eat tonight? I'd like to have the worth of it at those prices."

"Well, here's a little bit they won't get," Darrell said, putting a solid chunk into his mouth and chewing it up.

"How many did we get today, Gerard?" Perry asked.

"Close to 160. Half of them are pelted."

That took the taste off my fish. We ate all the hot supper, along with three loaves of bread. Then we indulged in the comforts of the galley for a few minutes. After Perry and Rodney shifted out to the wheel-house, we all filed out to face the pile of misery stiffening up on deck. Down the ladder, dress again, sweat again, battle into the repulsive blubber clothes again, pull on those cold bloody gloves again, and steel the bloody knife again. Eighty big, stiff, repulsive hulks lying on deck, pelted, washed, quartered and stowed, was worth sixteen dollars. "What a man wouldn't do for a buck or two," Randy said, pulling on his crispy, blubber clothes, looking at the heap of dead harps that lay tangled in a variety of death positions.

"My thoughts exactly," Paul replied.

Darrell pulled the plastic off a new pair of rubber pants, and before he got a chance to pull on his coat, Paul smeared the front and back with a bloody flipper. "Join the club."

He didn't resist the smearing saying only, "Yes. These are too clean for this job here tonight."

The plan was to off-load them all onto a pan, butcher and pelt them, pile the meat, and let the pelts, tied to a rope, soak in the sea overnight. Randy and Paul grabbed ropes and grapples and secured the long liner to a large, flat sheet about the size of a basketball court. The lights in the rigging lit up the whole pan. The pack ice was loose, see-sawing gently in the long, slow, swells.

It was a frosty night on the floes. At 10:00 P.M. we had them off-loaded and a few were pelted. The white sheet turned crimson and slippery. The wind was frozen to the pinnacles, the rain and snow stopped their attack on us and in the east a few frosty stars glinted in the sky. It was an eerie scene.

The seals were stiff, the fur matted and sticky. Razor-sharp knives gashed open large chests, spilling out still steaming entrails. Axes chopped and steam rose as men bent to the backbreaking work. Pelts were dragged, tied and tossed in the sea. Unbidden, my thoughts turned to polar bears.

I straightened out my breaking back and looked around me at the floes. Everything was a moving mass of shadows. If there were a thousand bears out there, zoomed in on the scent of blood and guts, I wasn't going to see them. The men worked steadily in the frosty night. In the glare of the lights they looked like they were smoking. The pile of old dogs was dwindling; a larger pile of meat was stacked and cooling, a polar bear's dream. No one else seemed the least bit concerned.

The cloud cover broke up and the arctic gave a spectacular display of beauty to anyone who turned his eyes skyward. A frosty "fingernail" moon, the blazing Hale-Bopp comet, the dancing northern lights, the magnificent Milky Way and galaxies of brilliant, glinting stars competed with each other for my attention. I recorded the beauty of it, decided that it was definitely a "plus," and bent back to my sculp.

It was 1:00 A.M. by the time we got it all sculpted, strapped, cleaned, stowed and secured for the night. We were all sore, tired and dirty. In the galley, over mugs of steaming tea, some of us did lighten up a little.

It started when Gerard said, "I have some good news and some bad news. The good news is, tomorrow we each get a shower and a change of underwear." Everyone brightened up.

"About time!" Paul said, "A week is long enough to go without a shower. What's the bad news?"

"The bad news is," Gerard replied, "Paul, you change with Darrell. Darrell, you change with David, David, you change with Randy…." We all burst out laughing. We chuckled all the way to the forecastle and we chuckled while we smeared on A-535. We chuckled between the moans and groans and the lamentations.

TUESDAY, APRIL 15

"Security. Security. Security. Marine weather forecast issued by Environment Canada for Tuesday, April 15...gale warnings issued for the east coast...Funk Island Bank...." The chuckling petered out to silence.

At 6:00 A.M. the captain's voice entered the forecastle. "Time to get up boys, and put down the fat." I came out of my sleep through a cloud of dread realizing what lay ahead. "Oh God! If I can live to get in out of this! Never again! This was the worst, the dirtiest, the hardest torture I've ever had to endure! Never again!" The thought gave me strength to groan out of my tomb, after Paul cursed every seal that had ever touched water all the while it took him to dress. Then I remembered. I had said the same thing a million times last spring, and the spring before that and all the other springs I hated to remember. I had to be a barbarian, a Viking or something. No, it was money that got me out here or, more like it, the lack of it. I fell back in bunk again.

Curse it! I'm going to be last one on deck this morning, I thought. Darrell got out like a cat, tutting sporadically. Randy "boy-oh-boyed" forty times, David tried to roll over. Nobody sang. I laboured out and followed suit. Perry, as usual, was in his chair, head down, reading the Bible or some other book. He did not look up when I passed him by. I realized then that while I reneged in bed, I had not heard him speak to anyone. It didn't matter. If he did speak to me the only acknowledgement I'd be able to make after I glanced at the rain-spattered, snow-laden windows, would have been a disgusted shake of my head.

Hot water revived me, breakfast satisfied me, dressing depressed me, opening the door disgusted me, reaching for my cold, sticky blubber clothes revolted me, the elements assaulted me, the sight of piled, frozen carcasses on a blood-pan the size of a basketball court, in the glare of the floodlights, turned my guts to the pit of my stomach. This was going to be another horrendous, rotten, miserable, eternal old day. The darkness retained its glory, the moon was frozen between two high pinnacles. Beauty and the beast. Gerard was setting up the winch and soon the first string of ten dripping pelts were hoisted down into the hold for Paul and Darrell to stow. When the last had been yanked from the sea, we turned our efforts to the two heaps of carcasses.

Randy and I plucked the frozen bodies from the pile on the bloodpan and loaded them into the net-bag, the winch pulling them aboard. *Yes sir, yes sir, twenty bags full.* We made ready to board the boat.

Randy was ahead of me. Stepping into a frozen pool of blood at the edge, he disappeared beneath the slob between the hull and the pan. In an instant, he surfaced with a gush of air and I pulled him out. He was dripping wet and white as a sheet when I helped him over the rails. Stripping off his clothes while he hopped about the deck, he disappeared inside. The Volvo roared and with a cloud of black smoke and soot that engulfed us, the long-liner crashed forward determined to get to the heart of the herd somewhere ahead.

While Gerard and I waited for Paul and Darrell to stow the pelts below, we quartered up the large carcasses. Gerard used the meat hook to pull the body across the chopping block where I chopped it into chunks. This was gory work with blood and meat fragments spattering everywhere. Finding it difficult to maintain stability on the shifting deck, I knelt down and soon I was engulfed in repulsive carcasses. I felt sick. Just before I thought I'd throw up, the last one was quartered. Then Paul came up from the hold with sweat dripping down his face, and in a scurry, ran to the rail, unclasping his clothes.

"Darrell wants you, Mick."

The next hour was spent in the labours of stowing and icing meat and flippers, waiting for the dripping meat to stop raining down, pulling the slippery, black-oily chunks across my body, fighting with the meat and cradling it in my arms in an effort to get it into place; sweating, puffing, straining, cursing and swearing on the dirt of it all. "How can anyone eat the likes of that!" Finally the last revolting carcass was iced.

We were dripping blood when we came up from the hold into the elements. The rain that struck me could have washed me clean in no time but Gerard insisted I get the "hose treatment." In that short length of misery, my body temperature dropped from boiling to freezing. "Lift your arms, open your coat, turn around," Paul scrubbed and scrubbed. Finally he said, "You're good enough."

"Yes, good enough to be a popsicle," I said, stiffly walking towards the hydraulic lines where I knew I'd find some heat. Soon everything was sprayed and scrubbed clean and the deck looked brand-new. David poked his head out through the galley window; the smell of breakfast whisked past my nose.

"Breakfast for two when you're ready," he said.

"How's Randy?" Paul asked.

"Best kind. He's having a cup of tea now."

Battling out of my blubber clothes, I made haste to the engine room and its glorious heat, changing into dry clothes while I was there, feeling better instantly. After a hot breakfast, I felt ready for the deck again, despite the elements.

It wasn't busy and soon after I was suited up, the elements got the better of me. There was no shelter from the southeast winds that spit snow and sleet at us relentlessly. I watched Darrel's blubber clothes slob over while he huddled beside me. Every now and then I'd relinquish the hot pipes to someone and stroll about striking myself to get the blood pumping. No one knew why we were out here suffering this brutality. What we did know was as long as Perry was up there with the gun, we all had to be ready to run. He came down frequently to go inside to warm, snack, brood, listen and look to see who was where. Seldom would he speak to us and if he did it was only in passing. I sensed he was not a happy camper. The pressure was on him to get us in the fat to harvest our share.

Gerard was standing beside the speedboat watching the topping grind slowly by. Walking up beside him, I found partial shelter in its lee. Casually, I placed my chest against the gunnel. The hull struck a sheet with a solid smack that transferred through the speedboat, striking me in the solar plexus with a hard, penetrating blow. It sent me reeling across the lurching deck in a yelp of pain and it was all I could do to keep from falling down. Then, feeling my food rising with the retch, I vomited over the rail in violent spasms. Eyes watering, I left the rail and returned to the vacant hydraulic lines.

"You all right?" Darrell asked.

Clutching onto the pipe with my left hand, rubbing my chest with the other, I looked at him and said, "No! I'm not all right. If I was 'all right,' I wouldn't be here!"

"I hear you man," he replied.

As I stood there in the wind and the rain, watching the moving ice frosting, shaking my head at the thought of it all, a lump of frost replaced my hot breakfast and my skeleton rattled.

Bang! Bang! "Over the side, Mickey," Gerard said, reaching for the winch controls, "That's a big one."

With a groan and a deep sigh, I stiffly took down the gaff and waited for the big dog-hood to come into view. "An old dog-hood is the only thing that could lie on ice on a day like this," I thought. With a scrunch on the hull, I let go of the rail and cautiously approached the dead monster, striking three vicious "just-in-case" blows to his bleeding skull before attempting to rope him. The winch screeched when I jumped for the blubber tire. As I reached for the gunnel, the knot in the rope slipped and down I went. My greasy gloves grabbed the rail and, instinctively, I pulled my legs up—the effort nearly causing me to lose my grip. If I had bitten my fingernails the night before, I'd have been a statistic. Springing towards me after an eternity of kicking myself up with my knees bent, Gerard grabbed me under the arm and flicked me in over the rail.

Five minutes passed before I was the better of the fright I got. I steamed about the forehead and collar, shivered and shook everywhere else. "You had like to do it that time," Gerard said, tying on another tire.

"I wouldn't have done it by myself. Jesus Christ! Thanks Gerard."

"Any time."

I double-checked the knot he tied.

"What did he have for his breakfast, Gerard?" Perry asked, coming down with a film of ice covering his clean rubber clothes.

With a slash of his blade, Gerard opened the stomach and we all looked to see what spilled out. Distinguishing nothing familiar, he looked up and said, "Kentucky Fried."

With a laugh, Perry went inside to get warm. We rolled in the swell for half an hour, while he was inside. When he did come on deck with his hand and mouth full of food, he announced, "We're going south."

"The Cayman Islands, I hope, skipper," I responded. "I heard there was a herd of fur seals down there that needs culling."

"Not that far south," he sneered, "we're going where I should have gone in the first place. To the patch off Fogo. That's seventy miles from here." Climbing the ladder to the control booth he turned the bow around and we started to punch back over the same ice we had just punched through. That was demoralizing.

"Seventy miles!" Paul exclaimed. "The hunt will be over before we get there! What a waste of time! If we had've gone southern in the first place, we'd have a load by now. All the other boats are doing good."

"Well, we're on our way there now, Paul." Perry thought he was doing right. "Let's just hope there's a few left for us when we get there," Gerard said.

"A few! I'd say that wouldn't be much out. The killer is that a few is no good to me. I need more than a few. I'm going inside."

We all took off our clothes and went inside and it wasn't long before Perry came in and maneuvered us through the slackening floes with the controls in the wheel-house. I sat around the galley for a while, replacing my breakfast with toast and beans, soaking the toast in my tea to ensure that it did not scrape my throat. Morale was low. The thought of beating back over what we fought our way through for the last week caused us all to sway lifelessly with the beating the ice gave us.

In the bridge it was no better. Perry concentrated on avoiding as many lurching pans as he could while Rodney slouched in the rumble seat, stretched out with his feet on the console like Mr. Glum. The radio blared out the news of the day. I was tender as a boil from head to toe, sick of looking at sleet and ice. I made my way, between the lurches, to my bunk. I preferred to take the beating lying down. I stretched out knowing that the rifle could report at any time to summon me to deck duty.

There was no rest to be found. I was beat to a suave, tired and sore, cold and shrunken, and the sound of ice scrunching and banging next to me got on my nerves so much that I wrapped the pillow about my ears to block out the noise. It was no good. Shocks from the floes tossed me around so much that I had to hold onto the frame with both hands, all the while expecting a chunk to come right in bunk beside me. Before long I found myself in a fury, cursing away venomously to myself on the damnable ice.

An hour of it was all that my body could endure. Cautiously getting out, I made my way topside. The scene through the windows did nothing to lift my spirits. Squinting into the glare, all I could see was moving ice and slobby water through a lashing wind, mixed with slop snow and rain. The storm was ripping the ice-field apart, making the going for us easier, and Perry weaved our way south at a steady four knots. He didn't talk much; nor did Rodney. I stood around for a while watching it crash by. "Young harp, there," he said.

Through the gloom, I looked to see the black on white. Perry stopped the ship and grabbed up the rifle and bullets. "Every one counts," he said. My stomach turned.

Out from the galley filed the boys with "not-too-pleasant" looks on their faces. I followed Paul down the ladder into the heat of the engine room. "One seal!" he said, pulling on a heavy sweater. "We're stopping for one seal! It don't make sense. We shouldn't stop until we see at least a hundred!"

The hull lurched ahead and the Volvo roared as I cautiously pulled on my clothes. The rifle fired when I was battling on my crispy, blubber clothes. "Over the side, Mickey."

We plucked a scattered young harp from the floes during the course of the afternoon, just enough to keep my body temperature soaring and dropping about five times an hour.

Then, at five o'clock, we came upon a great herd of old harps. They stretched for as far as my watering eyes could see. The floes were alive with them. Perry didn't raise the gun. He wanted the young harps. I watched, in amazement, the activity surrounding me.

As many as ten seals infested the bigger sheets. Some scurried off as we crashed near them, others did not. Some of the old dogs fought vicious battles right beside us, crashing their weight together in great tremors of fat. Jaws gaped, sharp teeth bared and nostrils flared. Healthy females lounged about on their sides, heads and tails in the air, looking on. Numerous heads poked from the slob, some rising shoulder-high, to get a better look around. "No trouble to get a load here," said Paul, scanning the herd and tutting away to himself.

They stretched on and on and on in a northeast-southwest direction, numbering in the tens of thousands. I got sick of looking at them as the evening passed because we all knew that as long as there were old ones to be seen, there'd be no young ones to be had. It was enough to make anyone sick.

At 7:00 P.M. Perry either got tired of seeing us hanging around freezing or else felt the urge to kill something. He halted in the infested floes and then he and Randy let loose with the high powered-rifles. Heads dropped, blood flowed, seals scurried, spent cartridges bounced off the deck, and the smell of burnt gunpowder drifted in the wind. When the shooting stopped, we counted twenty-five dead. Not all dogs.

Darrell, Paul and I jumped into the gloom and rain with gaffs and hawsers to drag them together for the winch to get them aboard.

Approaching the first big male, I noticed wounds in its pelt from the fighting he had done. The pelt was a "number two" from the start. Others were molting, their fur rendering them almost valueless. "They're no good for nothing," Darrell called to Perry, plucking a handful of fur from the big harp's back, letting it blow away in the wind.

"Well, bring them aboard. Keep them separate in the hold. We'll dump them along with the meat if we get into the young harps."

"The worthless, bloody things," Darrell said, sticking the tine of his gaff into the spurting bullet hole in the skull and giving a great yank.

It took us an hour. The herd was aggressive, breaking the surface right beside me, behind me, in front of me, here, there and everywhere with chilling gushes of air that turned the wet hairs on the back of my neck into steel bristles. They bobbed in the water and climbed with incredible speed right in front of me. One I killed with the gaff. I regretted it as soon a I had it done. Four hundred more bloody pounds of worthless dirt. They didn't seem a bit afraid and I watched them closely all the while I gouled their dead. I could see the heap on deck from where I stood. The ship was settling with the weight and I found it easier to climb aboard. In a cloud of black smoke, and a crash of the bow, the blood-pans fell away astern.

"Wouldn't that turn your guts, now," I said, sitting on the rail, steaming about my neck and forehead, spattered with blood, looking at the pile of corpses.

"Unhook the hawser," Gerard said.

Pushing off from the rail, I climbed atop the heap to do the job, sinking-knee deep in the tangle of bleeding bodies. As I was reaching for the hawser, the hull ricocheted violently off a hard sheet, tossing me off the pile. The dead seals shifted and as I pulled my foot up to avoid twisting my knee, my foot slipped out of my boot and I was horrified to feel the cold on my naked flesh. "No, God!" To get my balance, I placed my bare foot atop a dead seal. The pile came tumbling down.

The fur felt warm and sticky and I glared down to see my white skin turning red. My main concern was getting my boot, and forgetting my bare foot, I attacked the pile of corpses where I thought my boot should be. They were heavy and hard to pull away and they kept filling the hole I made. The boys saw my plight and with grins on their faces, pitched in to help me shift the worthless, bleeding brutes. Finally, I spotted it and reaching down, grasped onto it and snatched it from the gore. The white inside liner was as red as the outside. Standing barefoot in it all, I pathetically turned the boot bottom up. Nothing ran out. The boys did a good job of keeping from laughing.

In the washroom, I washed the red from my foot to expose the blue. It wouldn't return to white. Warmed by the hot water and a cup of tea, I didn't feel much better. Between collisions, I pulled a plastic bag over my dry socks to keep the bloody boot-liner from soaking them.

Back on deck the butchery continued. Darrell wasn't too pleased. "The bloody things!" he exclaimed, slashing one open, giving no heed to a number one sculp. "It's bad enough when you think you're making a few cents. It makes me sick to know that it's worth nothing from the start and if we're lucky it will all be thrown overboard in a few days."

"Yes boy. That's hard conditions to have to work under, not that the conditions we are working under are not depressing enough," I replied, steeling my knife before pulling one from the pile and laboriously rolling it over. "I don't see how it don't make us puke up that good fish." When the cloud of pungent steam engulfed me, I almost did get sick. At times, handling the dirty thing alone, I'd find myself with my face close enough to the twitching black flesh that if I puckered my lips, I could kiss it. "Boy oh boy oh boy," was all I could say, over and over and over again and again. As I was separating a pelt from around the rear flippers with a slash of my blade, the hull struck a glancing blow, and stumbling, I slashed the blade of my knife across my rubber boot.

Swearing at the realization of what I had done, I lifted it to see the cut. It was no trouble to see the two-inch slash. "Oh no! I just cut my boot!"

"Is it the same one you lost in the seals?" Darrell asked.

"No, it's the other son of a bitch!"

"Well, I guess you'll be a 'two bagger,'" he said, grinning.

"It's a sea of heart-break," I dismally replied.

By the time we got the last revolting one finished, the sun and Randy and Perry were long gone for the day. We scrubbed the deck clean, then ourselves. Now both of my feet were red. Thoughts of how good my sleeping bag was going to feel fuelled me as I struggled out of my blubber clothes. A hot supper sent cravings for the bunk through me, but not until the dishes were washed and the galley swept and cleaned.

By that time almost everyone had made their way to their berths. Perry and Rodney were in the wheel-house when I passed through. The radio was alive with news of ships stuck fast, damaged hulls, plied rudders and pumps working overtime. "We might not be getting many seals but we're a lot better off then some of those fellows," Perry said, swiviling in his chair, adjusting the dial. I recited a saying to myself that I had often heard my father repeat: "More in distress makes misery the less." How true.

"Security. Security. Security. All stations, all stations. Marine weather forecast issued by Environment Canada for tonight and Wednesday, April 16...Funk Island Bank...gale force northeasterlies...shifting to moderate westerlies, twenty-five knots in the evening...temperatures around zero...."

"So much for a good day tomorrow," I said, my stomach tightening up. "It might be better in the evening."

"Yes. Once the weather breaks, we might get a few good days. It can't keep up forever."

"We can only hope," I replied. Rodney pulled back his feet and I wished him and Perry good night then disappeared down the ladder. Things were quiet in the forecastle; no one spoke while I pulled off my clothes to the roll of the seas and groaned my way into my small berth, finding the very comfort I knew would be there in that sleeping bag. The tiny cell was taking on the aromas of the the Hunt; smelly feet, stinking socks, sweat, farts, A535, blubber and grease all mixed into one. It was to be expected. Pulling the bag up over my nose I smelled myself and I shivered at the thought of the past day and the miserable one coming. Only forty-eight had been taken all day. Twenty-five of them were all but worthless. Hopefully, we'd have to throw them overboard to make room for the young harps that were still thirty-five, ice-crusted nautical miles away, the journey toward which would start before first light regardless of the elements, start with the first *bang!* to get up. We burned down for the night, after a long, cold, frustrating, arduous old day, amid a civil ice-field, in two-metre swells, ninety nautical miles northeast of nowhere, with the pack gnawing to get in.

Wednesday, April 16

Bang! It was getting up time. Wednesday morning had arrived and the charge to the south continued with a crash and a lurch and a shiver through the hull that reverberated up my sore spine. Every collision maltreated me, every lurch hurt me all the while I lay there dreading to get up, cowering from the endless hours of bitter cold, wind, and slicing rain.

Gerard escaped up the ladder. Moans, groans, laments and complaints came from all directions. When the stem brought up solid, the skipper reversed the throttle and I begrudgingly threw off my warm sleeping bag.

Gerard was in the captain's chair when I passed through the wheelhouse on through to the washroom. There, the hot water and toothpaste lifted my spirits a little. The thought of my greasy, crispy blubber clothes and the hole in my boot took the taste off my breakfast. I fished two plastic bags out of the locker and made my way to the noise and heat of the engine.

While I was looking pathetically at the cut, Gerard passed me some glue. "Clean it with warm soapy water and apply this. Let it dry for ten minutes and you shouldn't have any trouble," he said.

"Thanks, Gerard," I replied.

Taking extra care, I followed his instructions and by the time I was suited, the heavy pelts had been thrown down in the hold. To escape the harsh elements, I went down with Paul and Darrell. It wasn't long before we had the repulsive things stowed. The pound was almost full and I had to crawl in atop them and pull the heavy pelts over me, then crawl out from under them to get them stowed. We worked like dogs knowing that if we were lucky, the worthless ones and all the meat would be left on a pan for a polar bear's feast. I almost lost my breakfast.

By dinner time the weather had eased up a little and visibility had increased. The going was slow and hazardous, the ice-field constantly moving and shifting on the three-metre swells. If the seals were as plentiful as the collisions, we'd all be millionaires even at eight cents each. But they weren't. Nine young harps were cooling and the floes were tightening up.

We ricocheted our way through another huge herd of adult harps, miles and miles of big, healthy fish-eaters in a frenzy of activity. They seemed to sense the fact that they were of no value to us and they lay about as we crashed by. Darrell sprayed a few close ones with the hose. Some faced us with jaws agape, challenging us. "Wouldn't that turn your guts!" he said.

We made steady progress through the herd and as the evening progressed, left it behind. I spent most of my time huddled by the hydraulic lines, my life support system, enduring the elements, trying my best to keep my skeleton intact. Perry was at the controls atop the wheel-house and Randy was having a scattered shot. "Come up and try your eye," Randy called.

Not only was every seal not killed immediately, a good many were shot in the back. It was a familiar scene among us sculpers on the aft deck. We joked that the pelt was not spoiled, it just had a buttonhole. For a change of pace, I climbed the ladder and stood in the wind next to the gunning table. "One over there," David called down from the spar. Perry crashed our way to within sixty yards and stopped the ship. Shouldering the rifle on the gunning table, I focused the cross-hairs on its head. My eyes watered with the wind and my bare hand burned with the cold while I waited for the right instant to squeeze the trigger. At the report of the rifle, the seal's head dropped immediately. A cloud of black smoke engulfed us when Perry gunned the throttle and Paul jumped to drag him in.

In the course of the next perishing hour spent bearing the brunt of the blistering wind, I shot nine more harps, all cleanly in the head. The next one we approached was partially hidden from my view by a small clump. I fired, and missed. Reloading, I focused on it scurrying towards the edge and fired again, stopping it dead.

When we approached it, we noticed it was not shot in the head. Perry shifted the lever to neutral, and stomped out of the booth. Assuming an arrogant stance, he glared at me and said, "That pelt is spoiled! You shot that in the back!" Turning away, he shouted to Paul to leave the seal and come aboard. Then he disappeared down the ladder into the wheel-house.

I was surprised and hurt. Wallowing there in the swells, looking around at the floes and the crew waiting, I felt bad. "Don't worry about that," Randy said. "That's not the first one that was shot in the back and it won't be the last, either. Perry gets mad at me like that all the time."

"Well, it's the first time for me and to tell you the truth I don't know what to think of it. Nobody says anything when *he* shoots them in the back. I've pelted a good many in the last week that were 'number twos.' What's the big deal? And to leave it on the pan when Paul was already out there don't make sense."

"Don't worry about it."

We rolled in the swells, dead in the water for twenty minutes, before Rodney came up and assumed the controls. He avoided looking at me when he said to Randy, "Dad is fuming down there now. He got no one to shoot, he got no gunners, and he got no one to steer. He got to do it all himself."

He finished with a shake of his head. I looked him in the eye and said, "Rodney, when I fire another shot from the bridge of this ship, it will be in self-defence." Then I turned and went back down to the deck and the hot hydraulic lines.

It did nothing to make my day to say the least. The boys just milled around waiting for the report of the rifle. Darrell came over and tried to cheer me up. "Don't let it bother you," he said, "Perry gets like that when he's under pressure. A hole in the back don't mean much. If that was the only one."

"Funny thing," Paul interjected, "When he shoots them in the body, he always got an excuse; it was the bullet, or the sleet or the ice or something else. Then, when you make a buttonhole, he got to get on like this. It don't make sense."

"What sticks in me," I replied, "is the way he said it. Just like he was scolding a little boy. It surprises me and says a lot about him."

"I'll venture to say that before this trip is over, you'll learn a lot more."

Perry came out on deck eating an apple, and without speaking, went up the ladder to the top deck. We meandered about waiting for the call to arms. The evening improved as it passed and our headway was a steady three knots. The engine slowed to idle. "Another one," Darrell said. *Bang! Bang! Bang!* "Over the side, Mickey."

"Say it while you can, Gerard, because once this one hits the dock, you'll never get to say it to me again." I said reaching for the gaff.

"Why? You're poisoned with it , are ya?"

"That's an understatement, Gerard."

"I know how you feel."

My enthusiasm was gone. I did the work as it came but my heart wasn't in it. I skipped across the treacherous floes to retrieve my tows but nothing invigorated me. I froze and thawed time and time again as the minutes slowly melted by. I accepted the dangers, coped with the merciless elements, and strained at the repulsive butchery but I didn't like abuse. I resigned myself to the fact that I would say nothing this time. I guessed he thought he had the most to lose in this venture. He likes to puff out his chest like the rest of the successful skippers and brag about all the seals he gets.

At 8:30 P.M. Perry came down and went inside with the rifles. We washed the deck and sprayed and scrubbed each other down before taking off the blubber clothes for the last revolting time. The sun was swallowed in a blaze of crimson-red cloud cover that heralded a good outlook for tomorrow. Red sky at night. That lifted my spirits somewhat as did the hot wash and the filling lunch David had prepared for us. After that I went to my bunk. Neither Perry nor Rodney spoke to me when I passed through the wheel-house.

Perry's face was in my face almost all night. I wished the Hunt were over. I was getting fed up with it all and now it seemed to me that he was blaming us, the crew for his problems. Once Darrell told us he had heard Perry mutter, after the radio seals had finished flying for the day, "Keith got the crew. He'll get the seals." That was bull. Like Paul said, "We can't get' em until we see em." My stomach turned the grating sound of ice against the hull was getting on my nerves. We tallied forty-five for the day. Fourteen hours in a freezer, one hundred nautical miles from land for nine dollars. I let out a moan and tried not to think of the oncoming day that would start with stowing down the fat and meat. Some degree of comfort came to me when I told myself again, "If I live to get in out of it, I'll never be caught out here again." Never again would I endure the miseries of the Hunt. I'd steal first. Sick and sore, bruised and abused, my body pulsing with throbs and aches, knees too tender to touch together, with feet that would not warm up, I nurtured that thought until I fell asleep. *Thump! Zzzz.*

Thursday, April 17

Perry roused Gerard out at 5:00 A.M. with a solid blow to the hull next to his ear. Lying there, feeling like an exhausted old man, absorbing the shocks and grinding my teeth, I visualized Perry at the helm, steering the hull at the rock-hard sheets, aiming to make them strike against Darrell's ear, his face drawn up in a sneer, saying to himself, "Here's one for you, Darrell. Get up out of bed! And here's one for you, David!" *Bang!* "No one stays in bed on this one while I'm at the helm!" In my groggy mind I saw him push himself forward for added momentum, relishing in knowing how uncomfortable it was for us in the bow. I snarled out of my bunk after a dozen smacks.

Through the windows, the dawn was but a hint on the horizon. Gerard was in the captain's chair. I sat in the rumble seat and held on to watch the dawn coming quickly to the tight ice-pack which begrudgingly gave us way at a rate of 1.2 knots.

Paul, driven from his berth by a solid blow to the starboard hull, came up the ladder in a frenzy, pulling on his T-shirt in the wheelhouse. Glaring about, he snarled, "I wasn't much out when I predicted a full week of being beat to death by the ice, was I?"

"No, and you weren't much out about the seals, either," I replied.

"A bit of breakfast might cheer me up some," he continued. "Ham and eggs. Will I fix some for you men?"

"Yes, an order for each of us," Gerard answered. Paul made his way to the galley.

By the time the call for breakfast came, the sun was breaking through the topping in all its blazing glory. It was going to be a great sealing day somewhere.

We were just sitting down at the table when the ship stopped and we heard the muffled reports of the rifle. "Let's go out, boys," Gerard said, pushing away from the table.

"I'm not going out there until I get my coat and boots," I said, shifting out behind him. By the time I got to the engine room and on deck, Gerard was standing up on a shifting ice-pan wearing deck shoes, jeans, and a T-shirt, with a dead seal hooked in his gaff. To my knowledge, this was his first time off the boat. The look on his face told me he wasn't contesting for "Mr. Congeniality." Passing the end of the gaff to Paul, who stood on deck wearing a T-shirt, jogging pants and sneakers, Gerard bent down, and grabbing the hind flippers, tossed as Paul pulled. It didn't come cleanly in over the side. It struck the gunnel and the shock caused a spurt of steaming blood to spatter over everything, including Paul.

Realizing he was spattered, he threw the seal and the gaff to the deck, causing another spurt of blood that rotted his sneakers. Mad as hell, he looked down over himself as the Volvo roared, "Christ, I'm rotted! It's not sensible! One lousy seal and I got all my clothes spoiled." Blood spattered his face, front and naked arms. He looked at me standing there dressed in my rubber boots with not a speck of blood on me. "Don't you laugh!"

To say the least, it took the taste off the nice hot breakfast we had left on the table. By the time we got back inside, it was all cold. Paul dominated the conversation. "One lousy seal!" he spat, pouring ketchup over his congealed eggs, "one lousy seal! Ten friggin' cents and I spoiled a hundred dollars' worth of clothes. It's not sensible!"

"What happened?" Randy asked, coming into the galley.

Paul told him the story, and as he venomously described the part where he got spattered, I burst out laughing and it wasn't long before we were all chuckling away at Paul's expense. "Too bad I never got it on the video. We'd be sure to win the ten thousand dollars," I said. "Especially with the look on your face when you threw it all down on deck."

The dragger slowed and all went silent while we waited for the shot. *Bang! Bang!* "Over the side, Mickey," Gerard said, "number two is waiting for you."

"You're a slave-driver, Gerard."

The day got better as it progressed and soon we were busy enough retrieving and sculping seals. Paul and I took turns of ten jumps each and by 9:00 A.M. we had fifty cooling.

Something was going on. The bullets Perry was using were not doing the job. Time and time again the seals came to life on deck while we scurried to sculp them. A sure sign of a bad shot was evident when we pelted the skin from the head. If the skull was intact it meant a lingering death from suffocation under the pile of corpses or from loss of blood. We were sick of having to kill the pathetic-looking things when they reared their heads and looked at us. It was gross and inhumane.

"Perry. Perry," Gerard called. "Those bullets are not doing the job."

"What's wrong with them?"

"You're not killing them. It seems that the bullets are passing on through or bouncing off the skull. We're sick and tired of having to put them out of their misery."

"That's why you have a hakipik, isn't it?" he replied curtly, turning his back to us. I suspected I knew what the problem was and it made no sense to me in light of the fact that we paid top prices for the best of ammo. It was appalling, unnecessary carnage.

One beater among the pile lifted its head and started to scratch his way around, his eyeballs two swirling pools of blood. His lower jaw was hanging down from his mouth by a thread of skin. "Darrell, kill that, will you?!" Gerard said.

Grabbing the hakipik, he did not kill it immediately. Instead he pressed the wooden handle up against the top teeth of the suffering creature. "Bite that if you can." The poor thing had no bottom teeth and all it could do was crawl around in the swath.

"I said kill it, not play with it!" Gerard roared, snatching the pik from him and dispatching it with three vicious blows to the head.

The harp suffered no more. I was sick to my stomach. Another seal I spotted in the heap, its eyes reflecting the life that lay within, reminded me, for some reason or other, of my father. Shaking my head at the cruelty of it all, I killed it with the hakipik.

The ice-field was loosening up and we could pretty much steam where we liked. It was slippery early in the morning but as the hours passed, I'd sink deeper and deeper into the rotting crust each jump I made. The long, slow, three-metre swells kept everything in motion.

Rodney came down from atop the wheel-house to get warm, saying to David, "Dad is up there grumbling about how dirty the washroom is. He told me to tell you to clean it up."

While we were huddled together, Gerard told us a story about a man from his hometown that Gerard had heard complaining about his wife. "I can't never get nuttin' off Nelly. She's always got an 'in-fact-ion!" The way he said it made even Rodney chuckle before he went inside in the warm. He wore coveralls just like his father.

Without delay, David got the detergents and did the job. Just after he had finished, Randy came down and shucked off his blubber clothes. "Nature calls." Twenty minutes later, he returned to the deck, scratching his crotch.

"What, did you catch the crabs, Randy?" Darrell asked.

"No," he replied, "David cleaned the toilet with detergents. My privates touched the bowl and the chemicals burned me," he replied, scratching and grimacing at the same time. "Don't say it's not bad!"

"Everyone stay away from Randy," Darrell declared, "he's got an 'in-fact-ion.'" We all chuckled away at that and Randy battled on his soiled rubber clothes saying, "Don't laugh. It could have happened to you."

By 10:00 A.M. the quarry was plentiful. Working in the gore when I wasn't jumping, I frequently saw three and four young harps sleeping around us. Conditions were ideal when the skipper gave orders to ready the speedboat for launching. Looking at me, he asked, "Will you go with Randy?"

"Yes," I replied.

It took no more than ten minutes to get ready. That's the thing about the Hunt, everything is done in short order. Soon I was sitting on the forward tot of the *Blue Dolphin*, filling the magazine with five rounds of ammo, with Randy closing the distance on a sleeping young harp. The ice was tighter then the last time with leads of open water. The "nobby" rubble nearly beat me to pieces, as I crouched there watching the harp that had not yet raised its head. In the cross-hairs, I could clearly see the back of its skull. Randy was keeping a steady course; the boat was his bullet. Glancing ahead the bow I saw clear water coming. Pressing the rifle into the lifejacket, I didn't wait for him to awaken. Fur and smoke puffed from the skull and a shock wave rippled down his neck. Other then that he didn't move. Putting my .222 Remmington in the rack, I turned to Randy by the engine. "When I got to go, I hope I go as quick as that."

"Yes, sir."

Keeping the ship within view, we cracked it to them without mercy. One time we stopped and killed four on one pan with three more watching a hundred yards away. One was hit in the back and as I tossed him aboard, Randy saw the wound. "A button-hole for the skipper," he chortled.

"Right on."

"Do you see the boat?" he asked.

"Yes," I replied, "over there about a mile." We watched her and noticed that she was "dead in the water." No smoke belched from the stack. We made our way over.

Long faces greeted us as we approached the crippled ship. Perry came to the rail with a wrench in his hand, asking how many we had, not looking too well-pleased.

"Around thirty," Randy answered. "Do you have trouble?"

"Yes, the steering line is broke but there's nothing you can do to help. Get them unloaded, the day is passing fast enough!" With the wrench in his hand, he returned to the ruptured line.

"Thirty-three seals in ninety minutes," Randy stated when the last one went in over the rail. No one seemed impressed. We had time enough to grab a tin of drink and a couple tins of sausages, then we were off into the floes again, leaving the crippled swiler wallowing lifelessly. No one waved us off.

Soon we had a target in sight and the thrill of the Hunt invigorated me. I wasn't hungry, I wasn't cold and I wasn't tired. To kill a boatload was our objective and we went at it in earnest. By the time we had the bottom covered, we saw the *C. Michelle* belching to life again and intermittent, muffled reports of gunfire resounded across the floes. The glint burned my eyes and blurred my vision. For relief, I reached down and soaked up hot blood with my fingers, smearing it on my cheekbones. It dried quickly to my face. I felt the relief immediately and looked back at Randy. "My God! You don't look cute!" he said when he looked at me.

"Cute is not a factor out here," I replied, "just as long as it keeps away the snow-blindness. I'm not entering any beauty contests."

Forty seals later, Randy was cold and uncomfortable back by the engine and we yearned for a cup of tea. Chilled to the bone and starving, we worked our way towards the ship. Within three hundred yards, Perry approached the rail.

"How many do you have?" he asked in a not-too-happy-to-see-us-tone.

"Close to forty," Randy replied.

"Why did you come back?"

"Because I'm hungry and cold and I want to use the washroom and get a cup of tea," Randy stated.

"Well, make it quick!" he replied. "Boys, unload those seals, we're losing the best part of the day." I noticed that he looked strangely at me and I realized why when I glanced in the mirror while I was washing, reminding myself to get my sunglasses.

It was four o'clock by the time I had hastily eaten my lunch and changed into dry clothes to protect me from the evening chill, knowing this time we would not be back until dark. When we returned to the deck to battle on the blubber clothes, the harps were in a heap and Perry was in the speedboat, bailing out the blood. He scampered in over the rail and untied the painter. I pushed off from the hull and readied the rifle. It was good to be away from the ship. "One over there." *Bang!*

Our quarry got scarcer as the sun sank lower and the temperature dropped. Standing on the forward tot in the wind as we banged our way through the practically deserted ice scape, I soon got very cold. The last hour seemed like a long time to kill three. In the glow of twilight, we approached the glaring mast lights of the long-liner.

"I'm having a cup of tea before I touch any of these seals," Randy said, steering us closer. "I'm nearly frozen to death."

"I'm perished, too, but I'm not taking off these blubber clothes until the last thing is done for the night supposing it kills me."

"How many do you have?" Perry asked.

"Over forty."

"Get them unloaded, then," he said turning away and going inside. The winch sounded and we mixed our forty-four in with the thirty-five on deck, making a huge heap of bloody harps.

Making room beside Darrell, I steeled my knife and picked one from the pile and turned it belly-up, between my feet. Bending over and placing the razor-sharp edge of my knife against his bottom lip, I slit him open from tongue to tail. The intestines spilled out and a cloud of steam engulfed me. I slashed open the ribcage and grabbed the sticky entrails, just as Gerard, Darrell, and Paul were doing.

We were served sandwiches and juice at ten o'clock and I bolted mine down with blood-crusted fingers. My back was breaking and I wasn't sure what was cracking more: my blubber clothes or my joints. I was crimson with blood that, at times, sloshed halfway up my boots. My breath mixed with the pungent steam rising about my face and each time I bent over, I doubted if I'd be able to straighten up. No one sang, no one laughed, no one played around. Other than the frequent sounds of knives rubbing steel, only the ice was heard. Pick another one from the pile. Roll it over on its back, hunch up my shoulders then bend over, clothes cracking while I make the initial cut. Steam rising in my face, trying not to breathe, trying not to slip, watching out for geysers. Reaching in to grab the windpipe, blood dripping off my knife. Brothers staring at me from the heap, big black lifeless, glazed eyes. That one has a glimmer of life. Shade my knife and grab the hakipik. *Smack, Scrunch, Mush.* How much, in the name of God, is this worth an hour?

It was 10:30 P.M. before Darrell sculped the last, stiff one, bringing the tally for the day to 330. We then loaded the speedboat and washed and scrubbed it all clean. The deck was washed clean and then the final freezing of the day came when Paul told me to step forward for rub-down. "Put up your hood, turn around, lift your arms, open your coat…." *Brrrrrrr.* Finally, I was clean enough to stiffly and thankfully battle out of the revolting things for the last time that day. Without the least bit of reluctance I closed the door on all the cold, dreads, dangers and death that dwelled out there in abundance.

A hot wash cleaned me a little and a lunch revived me enough to get to the forecastle and the moans, groans and grumblings that abounded there. Paul was most unhappy. "If we had've gone southern with the rest of the boats, we'd have a load now."

"If we never had steering trouble today, we'd have another eighty for sure," replied Darrell.

"If your aunt had testicles, she'd be your uncle," Gerard piped up. "By the way, Randy, how's your "in-fact-ion?" Randy didn't reply. Soon the tiny space quieted. "Security. Security. Security. Marine weather forecast for Friday, April 18…Funk Island Bank…gale to storm force northerlies…rain and slop-snow…." Groans and moans came from all around.

I lay in my bunk acutely aware of every joint in my body. I had never felt this way before. I ached, pained and spasmed all over. It seemed to take all my effort just to shift my bony legs into a fetal position. The hull rolled and rocked in the long swells and Beethoven nudged the hull. Totally exhausted and sore from head to toe, I succumbed to the sandman at midnight, sixty miles southeast of the Funks, too tired for even my mind to wander.

Beethoven and my sore body denied me rest. I felt every nudge the floes made. The sandman must have sprinkled some in my eyes because they kept watering and paining each time I closed them. Everyone else seemed to be resting uncomfortably.

Friday, April 18

At 4:00 A.M., I heard the generator start, heralding in the blusterous, miserable day, bringing my thoughts to 330 corpses and 660 flippers that needed to be lifted, shifted, dragged, lifted, dropped and shifted, lifted, dragged, stowed, and iced in the pounds. I let out a long, mournful moan and concentrated on getting to sleep. I had to sleep! It didn't seem long before the captain's voice entered the forecastle. " Time to get up, boys."

The weather was as horrible as was predicted and I received the cruel lashing from Jack Frost as I followed the procession back and forth. "Hold up!" Darrell shouted from below. I waited in the cold for them to do their work.

The hold was as revolting as I knew it to be and I was ringing-wet with sweat before the final grisly carcass was gaffed into place and iced over with the last of our ice supply. Before getting in for breakfast and a change of clothes, I did a half-hour "turbulent-time" on a tossing ice-pan in the rain, loading heavy chunks of ice, followed by a turn kneeling amongst it, breaking it up with the back of the axe. By the time I finished "scrub-down" at 10:00 A.M., I was frozen and thawed a dozen times. My tender body hardly knew if it was coming or going.

While we were eating breakfast, Perry came into the galley and said, "Boys, I just heard on the radio that the harp quota closes tomorrow evening at dusk."

"Great," responded Paul. "We haven't seen any yet!"

"How many do we have aboard?" Perry asked Gerard.

"Close to a thousand," he replied.

"Not a lot, is it boy?"

"No sir, it's not."

"Well, we did the best we could. Maybe I should have gone southern but I didn't know. Anyway, there it is and it closes tomorrow evening. We'll pick up as many as we can." Turning away, he went outside.

"By the looks of things, we won't get many today. We'll be lucky to make up a thousand. That's makes for a pretty poor trip. Two weeks of this and about four hundred dollars to show for it."

"You haven't got a cent, yet," Darrell corrected him. "We're not in yet."

"Four hundred dollars," Paul continued, "I know people who pay more than that for a wash, a shave, a manicure, and dinner!"

"It's not very much," Randy confirmed. "It's no harm to say, sealers earn their meagre pay." The Volvo roared and the hull crashed forward and we all paraded out to get ready for deck duty.

It wasn't fit for a seal to lie on the ice. We hung around waiting for something to happen, in the wind and the rain and the misery. It was warmer in the water today. The dragger stopped. *Bang!* "Over the side, Mickey."

"That's easy for you to say, slave-driver."

Perry battered our way to the south adamant on reaching the elusive main patch, the same one we had sought for the last two weeks. No one was in very good spirits. It was a disappointing spring with about one third of the pounds full and one seal on deck with thirty-three hours left to make a few dollars.

Huddling by the hydraulic lines, my skeleton rattling inside my clothes, I was vaguely aware of Gerard coming down the metal ladder. Halfway down, the hull struck a sheet and the subsequent lurch threw him to my feet. It took both Darrell and me to get him back up. I thought he was killed. He wasn't but he had hurt his ribs and his knees. "F— this," he bellowed a few decibels lower than the roar of the Volvo.

I was glad this misery was coming to an end and I wished there were thirty-three seconds left, not thirty-three hours. Time passed like the melting of ice with only enough seals to soar my temperature up so the wait could plummet it down. By three o'clock, we had eighteen pitiful sculps to show for ten hours' misery. I was nearly perished when David called, "Hot soup for two."

I battled my way out of my blubber clothes and after ten minutes beside the roaring main engine, I sat in for a bowl of hot soup. It was delicious and David poured me a second bowl. With that and a cup of tea, I was feeling a little better. It wasn't long before deck duty called me away from the galley. With a litre of liquid sloshing around in my shrunken stomach, I suited up, dreading the thought of all of it freezing.

Perry brought us upon another one and Darrell made the jump to warm himself up. It wasn't long before it lay on deck bleeding profusely. "He's your puppy, now," he said, when he laboriously climbed in over the rail. *Vrrooom!*

As I picked up my bloody knife and giving it a few rubs with the steel, my stomach gave an involuntary retch. The blood that sloshed about inside the steaming carcass reminded me of the soup that sloshed about in my stomach and beads of sweat broke out on my brow. By the time I had the thing butchered, I tossed the dripping entrails over the rail and with three violent convulsions, was sick to my stomach. Throwing down my knife, I assumed the position by the rail. Shrouded in oily soot and smoke, I was violently sick again. The elements showed no mercy. The ship struck a pan that almost threw me overboard and I grabbed on to the steel stabilizer cable to stay aboard. The end of the cable was frayed and a strand struck into the palm of my right hand. I felt the tingle of pain register and pulled my hand away. I felt the steel sliver withdraw from my flesh before I grabbed the gunnel. Gerard had my seal pelted before I could straighten up enough to hold onto the hydraulic lines. "Yes, it's enough to make you sick," Paul said, decapitating a carcass and throwing the head overboard. Two protruding, dead eyes stared at me before it disappeared. "It makes me sick."

If he was sick, it was a different sickness than from the one I suffered from. I couldn't do anything but hold on and watch the crew do the work. At 6:00 P.M., Gerard came up to me and said, "You're relieved of duty for the rest of the day. Go inside and get warm."

I didn't want to but knowing I was of no use to anyone, I complied with his order. "Gerard, I wouldn't leave if there were any seals."

"If there was any seals, you wouldn't be like this."

I felt like I was copping out. Reluctantly I shivered out of my blubber clothes and went inside. With no reason to rush, I luxuriated in the heat of the roaring engine room until the sweat was on my brow and my ears rang. I spent a half-hour in the washroom trying to straighten up using lots of soapy hot water and Crest. Along with the scourge of seasickness, I felt a pang of guilt for leaving them. The intermittent report of the rifle and the working of the ship made me feel worse.

I made my way to the galley and sat at the table, resting my head on my arms, lifelessly rolling with the punches. My growling stomach told me I should eat but my body begged me not to move. I felt every shift of the ship and from time to time, over the roar of the engine, I heard the voices of the men working. I pictured exactly what was going on out there in the wind and rain and the oily smoke: waiting for the rifle to fire, to see it lying there; one seal on a moving pan, fifty yards away. It would make anyone sick to have to jump and land and hop and skip and jump for their very life, just to drag back one seal and see it bleeding on deck. How could you not be sick to have to roll it belly-up between your feet? Then and there I prayed vehemently for an end to this. This was the worst! This would never happen again! *Bang! Bang!*

From out of the gloom came thoughts of my sleeping bag, and the overpowering desire to rest my throbbing head propelled me away from the table and down the ladder to the forecastle. The sight of my bunk gave me energy enough to groan my way in and I collapsed back upon the pillow. But the guilt really got to me. To be lying there looking at the light coming in through the skylight while the ship worked the floes made me feel like a wimp. I finally settled with the fact that I couldn't help it and that if it were busy, I wouldn't be here in bunk.

There was no comfort to be found but my spent body seemed to mold into the foam mattress but I knew this was the only place for me regardless of how bad it was. There was no let-up in the ship's assault and the time banged by.

An eternity later, I felt the ship stop and the engine die. It was eight o'clock and the day was spent. I got great relief in the stillness and quiet of the tiny room but it was overshadowed by the thought of the crew coming down and seeing me. I knew what was going on up there and I heard Perry shifting around in the wheel-house. That was the hardest part of it all—facing the men who had done all the repulsive labour.

From my berth, I could hear them in the galley getting lunch. The thought of something to eat sent a tumble through my empty stomach. I was hungry but not hungry enough to get up, pass through the wheel-house, along by Perry and Rodney sitting in the chairs, and into the galley and sit at the table amongst the crew. No way! Instead, I lay there, rubbing my growling stomach, dreading the first man to come down the ladder.

They all seemed to come down together and within a few minutes the place was a beehive of activity. Men quickly shed their clothes and crawled into their berths in a chorus of groans, moans, growls and curses. They inquired as to how I was and all I could say was, "You're iron men on a wooden ship."

The place quieted pretty quickly and in the darkness, I relished the comfort of the sleeping bag and the absence of ice crashing against the hull. It had not been a very productive day. We had culled the herd by only forty-four seals, bringing the total, according to Gerard, to 1,032, with one day left in the Hunt. By this time tomorrow evening, it would be history and it was going to be the last time I would subject myself to this misery. Four hundred dollars wasn't worth it. That would hardly cover the cost to replace the clothes and supply enough cleansers for me to get the foul smell of seal blubber out from the pores of my skin.

My knife hand, where the steel cable had punctured it, was bothering me as I lay there waiting to succumb. It was stinging and irritable and my fingers seemed to be stiffening up. Turning on my light, I focused my eyes on the palm of my hand. Despite the scrubbing I had given them, blood had seeped into my pores. The puncture itself showed up as a white spot about the size of a pimple. I feared blood poisoning and made a mental note to take extra good care of it, starting with new gloves first thing in the morning. Oh, the morning. Dreading the dawn, I drew the sleeping bag over my bony shoulders, tried to ignore the hunger pains and all the other pains. I concentrated instead on how nice it would be to crawl under the covers on my own bed at home and cuddle in beside my wife...with no ice gnawing at the walls and no swells rocking the bed. The thought of passing her a measley four hundred dollars killed the pleasantness of it all and with a long sigh, I relinquished myself to rest. "Security. Security. Security...marine weather forecast for tonight and Saturday...issued by...at 10:00 P.M. for Funk Island Bank...westerly gales, forty to fifty knots, mixed with rain and fog...shifting to moderate south-westerly, twenty to twenty-five knots in the evening...lows tonight, minus ten; highs Saturday two degrees...."

SATURDAY, APRIL 19

The final day of the remnants of the Greatest Hunt in the World started with a tremendous crash at 5:30 A.M. The shock jolted me awake, and emitting a long, woeful groan, I became aware of my sore body. The most overwhelming pain was that of hunger from my shrunken stomach, followed by the aching of my sore muscles and lower back. Grabbing the wooden framing, I felt the pain shoot from my punctured hand. Looking at it in the glare of the cabin light, I saw that the pimple had reddened and the flesh on the back of my hand was tight and swollen. A pang of dread mixed in with the pain—blood-poisoning!

Gerard escaped with his shirt in his hand. I took the beating for a little while but before long, I knew the time had come to face the day and I miserably crawled out of my warm sleeping bag. Grabbing new gloves, a clean face-cloth and towel, I followed Gerald's lead to escape the bombardment.

In the washroom, I took particular care to clean the wound. Through stabs of pain, I scrubbed and scrubbed the engrained blood from the infected area. I knew this was serious and my dilemma started. I was hoping for a job on this ship or another ship and I knew the rule was, "you're no good in bunk." I knew if I told anyone and the skipper had to abandon the Hunt to bring me in, it would not look good on my résumé. The only chance I had for work was to keep on working.

I ate a sparse breakfast, which stopped the growling. On deck it was foggy, cold, and miserable, exactly as I expected. Trying to make up for the lost time of yesterday, I lost no time digging into the pitiful pile of repulsive pelts lying on the stern. Grabbing one in each hand, I found it difficult to hold the weight in my bad hand and several times it slipped my grasp. Pain was shooting in my wrist. I was relieved to know Paul and Darrell were going to stow the meat before they came up.

As I drove my hand into a carcass, it slipped away and off came my glove. Before I got it back on, grease and blood covered my hand. There was no way to escape it, so I decided to say nothing and put up with it, although in the back of my mind, I wondered if it was the right thing to do.

I washed and cleaned it again before I ate my lunch at ten o'clock. It seemed to be getting worse and the swelling tightened the skin on the back of my hand. Every time I used it, it throbbed.

I was purely miserable, huddling next to the hot hydraulic lines, waiting for the report of the rifle. The crew all looked the same way. It wasn't fit to be out, but it was fit for a scattered few to lie, and eventually die, on the floes. *Bang!*

To tell the truth, it turned my guts to see one coming through the fog and the feel of the gaff-handle in my hand made me wish I'd never see another bloody seal. In less than an hour I had ten jumps in and they were crawling up all around us, oblivious to the wind and freezing rain. Drops of icy water mixed with my sweat, and frequently I had to remove my gloves to wipe it away. Each time I noticed the wound covered in filth and there was nothing that I could do about it. I had to work.

Pelting became difficult because I was unable to squeeze my knife tightly in my hand and several times the handle slipped from my grasp, slicing holes in the rubber gloves, through which the gore flowed.

By dinner-time, we had fifty sculps and the Hunt was heating up, dissipating the fog. The wind was abating and shifting to the southwest, shredding the ice pack. Visibility had increased to a couple of miles and the seals crawled up.

Randy came down off the top deck and with less than nine hours left in the Hunt, informed me that we were going out in the speedboat. I looked around at the foggy ice-field and a shiver ran down my spine. Even though I didn't like the look of it, I told him I would go with him and hastily we readied the *Blue Dolphin* for hunting. Within a few minutes, I was sat in the cuddy, loading my rifle with live ammo while Randy zig-zagged our way around most of the floes, bearing down on our first target. I kept a watchful eye on the ship hunting its way through the fog and drizzle. "Don't lose sight of that boat!" Randy stated.

Standing on the forward tot, grasping the taunt painter with my left hand, I could see far more fog and rain than Randy standing back by the engine. "I don't plan to," I replied. The harps appeared like rats, stretched out, balled up, crawling around, and scratching their way up. In the perilous drizzle, a mile from the ship, I again experienced the thrill of the Hunt and immediately I knew it was this feeling that kept me coming back, to speed through mirror-calm swatches sprinkled with rubble, the sound of it tinkling off the bow, vrooming my way past the larger pans peering in over to see our quarry stretched out. The wind seemed to incite me, and the feel of the gun and the sight of those watery eyes looking at me pumped me high. I could see for miles and miles. Everywhere I saw young harps. And we cracked it to them with everything we had, shooting to kill, taking no prisoners, showing no mercy, giving no pardon, seeking out and destroying as many as we could, as quickly as we could. Sometimes they lounged five and six in company, stretched out digesting our fish. Those that were awake watched us come within range. Sometimes I'd empty the magazine, scurrying to reload with three or four watching me. They'd escape if I missed my shot and the bullet sprayed ice over them. Even then, some would stop for that last fatal look, as if to see the bullet coming.

I didn't mind the wind rushing past and I hardly noticed it charging inside my coat through the busted zipper. Drizzle mixed with the sweat from the exertion of jumping out, running, vaulting, hooking and towing, lifting, tossing and jumping. *Vrrooom!*

Sometimes I had my bloody gloves on, sometimes I had to search for them. I was engulfed in the rush of the Hunt.

I was also battered about with the punching ice and numerous times I had to use my bad hand to save myself from being tossed overboard. I knew my hand was getting worse but I took consolation in the fact that there were only a few hours left and maybe by tomorrow night, I'd be in port and get medical attention. In the meantime, I got caught up in the heat of the Hunt, and searching out and shooting the young harps sequestered all queries from my mind and body.

The little boat soon felt the weight of its cargo and the water was but a few inches below the gunnel. I did not have to lift the heavy seals at all to get them aboard. Speeding through the stripped up pack with our quarry in abundance, I knew this was a part of the Hunt I'd miss in years to come. It was fast, dangerous and exhilarating work, the time sped by and the blood-pans fell astern.

The weather had improved and from atop the three-metre swells, I kept an eye on the mother ship. For the past while I had noticed no smoke smudging the drizzle and I commented to Randy that it looked like they had more trouble. We had a full load aboard, so Randy decided to work our way back towards her. The weight sunk us low in the water and I sat atop the tot watching the spray spit back over the stem. Sometimes when we sank in the troughs, I thought we were going to dive right in and time and time again I found myself unconsciously making the effort to will the bow upwards. Now, when we glanced off the pans, the bow struck with a solid blow that I feared would puncture the thin fiberglass. I wondered what I'd do if we started to sink.

Long faces met us again when we slowly approached the starboard side. Their attention was on a piece of the steering mechanism placed on the hatch. Perry came to the rail, " How many did you get?" I guessed he was not too well pleased.

"A full load," Randy responded, "We must have close to seventy."

"You shouldn't have come back yet," he blurted. "I've had as many as ninety aboard that one. Why did you come back?"

"Because we had a load," Randy said. "You might have had ninety in her but this is the most I've ever had aboard. By the way she was behaving, I wouldn't want to be aboard of it with ninety."

"Come on, let's get them unloaded! We're losing time! You shouldn't have come back yet."

I noticed Darrell favouring one hand and I asked him what was wrong. "I sliced open my finger with my knife. The boat struck a pan and I missed my mark. No more pelting for me."

I became conscious of my own hand and how sore it was inside my bloody glove, bathed in dirt and grease. I felt like saying, "Yes, and I got a bad hand too and I'm not pelting any more, either!" But I didn't. Instead, I said. "It don't surprise me that you slashed yourself open. I'll be even more surprised if one of us is not stabbed from the throwing around we get with sharp knives in our hands. I think we're lucky in that regard."

Within an hour, we had unloaded seventy-eight seals from the speedboat. No one was impressed. We gassed up the two tanks, replenished the ammo, and grabbed a lunch to go. Randy and I sped off with renewed vigour to finish the Hunt. No one waved us off. The best of the day was passed and soon fog banks obscured our view. The seals seemed to have rested and digested enough; most of them were wide awake and "yarry," forcing me to make longer shots. The rifle was true and we kept up a good EHA (earned harp average). We shot quite a few in the water. Smoke from the funnels assured us that the steering was fixed and scattered muffled rifle reports told us that the ship was back into the frenzy. With just three hours remaining, we sped through the knobby swells, one eye peeled for seals, the other on our mother ship feeding in the fog.

We passed one great ice pinnacle that stood eighty feet high and sent shivers down my spine. I called it to Randy's attention and asked him what it reminded him of.

Looking at the huge ice-sculpture that towered over us, he declared, "My God. It looks just like a man wearing a hooded coat, standing on the ice, frozen to death."

Both of us watched the frozen ice-man get swallowed up by the fog. Another shiver raced through my body and I looked around until I spotted the smudge of smoke.

The scarcer the seals got, the colder it got and soon my skeleton rattled and my teeth chattered as I stood on the greasy tot, in the brunt of the wind, scanning the lifeless floes.

Cruising down an open lake of water, I spotted two harps lying on a pan, two hundred yards into the rubble. I made motions to Randy, and he pounded our way through. The ice was heavier than we expected and it took us ten minutes to get within range for a shot. Several times pieces sunk beneath the bow and surfaced at the stern, pushing the prop clear out of the water. Randy would grab a gaff and push them away.

Three shots killed the two harps and while I was out retrieving them, I realized, with a cold chill of dread, that I could no longer see the boat. She was gone.

"Do you see the boat?" I asked apprehensively.

"No. Do you?"

"No."

"Oh no!"

Frantically we drove the boat back to the open lake, taking what seemed to be a very long time. Standing on the forward tot, frantically searching the foggy floes for the smoke, I was nearly tossed overboard a couple of times and only saved myself at the expense of grabbing the gunnel with my sore, throbbing hand. Back at the lake, we tried to construct where we had last sighted the ship but we were doubtful all the time. Everything looked the same, ominous and foreboding.

"Perry is working south," Randy said, standing on the centre tot. "Shocking to be out here with no compass."

"We don't have much time. We will soon have to look for a pan for the night. What a way to end the Hunt. Maybe we could tie up to that ice-statue we saw earlier."

"Shut up, Mick! Don't be talking like that. Fire that rifle, will you? If we can't hear them, maybe they will hear us. We got lots of bullets so if worst comes to the worst, we'll survive the night."

Firing three shots in the fog bank, we sat back and listened for a response. It was not a good situation, lost in a small open boat, in the floes, ninety miles off Cape Fogo. Soon the ice had surrounded us. The air was filled with the crunching sound of it gnawing at our hull and the eerie, chilling sound that a shifting ice-field makes as it eats itself. Looking at the pile of dead seals, I wondered what kind of bed they would make and for how long.

Hearing nothing but the grinding of ice, Randy started the engine and we crashed our way again to the shrinking lake of open water. After firing another three rounds, we sat quietly and strained our ears to hear something. It was a cold and anxious time and thoughts of death on the floes filled my mind. You don't die on the ice, you perish.

The piercing wind caused me to turn about. Was she over there? Or was she somewhere over there? It all looked the same to me, gloomy white, misty and foggy, dismal and threatening and very, very intimidating. Large chunks of mean-looking ones encroached upon us. Before long it had us surrounded again, nibbling all around, loud enough to drown all other sounds. Two seals came out of the drizzle. I didn't even mention them.

Randy scratched himself and gazed around, listening as intently as I. "We shouldn't be let go the rail without a compass. I know Glen would take the one off the bridge and give it to ya before he'd let us go off clear the boat," he said in a helpless-sounding voice and a worried looked on his face. There was now no water in sight, just white. "I'm steaming up here aways until we finds a lead. We'll fire a few shots and wait for a spell. If we don't hear nothing, we'll find a low pan big enough. We'll unload the seals, and I'll beach this one with the engine. Then…we'll see." Lifting the gas can, he said, "We got about half a tank. How many bullets you got?"

Counting the bullets, I told him we had two-and-a-half boxes. Fifty rounds. *Vroooom!!* The Enduro fired to life with six inches of cord. The push through the floes was barbaric. The rubble compressed to a thick mulch that required almost full throttle to push apart and which swallowed our wake within twenty yards of the stern. Half a tank—thirty minutes; and we needed some for a fire. Through the drizzle and milky white we spotted the darker dismal-grey of a berg. Its passage through the floes, or the floes passing by it, left a small open swatch. Randy pounded our way to the clear water wake of the gigantic cathedral, enormous enough to awe men as big as the ice statue. As handy as we dared, he shut down the engine.

It was ominously quiet. We could see for yards and yards except for where the berg blocked our view. The seas lapped at its pearly white foundation, and water droplets dripped in the smooth sea all around, making the only sounds I heard. Even the floes were quiet as if awed into silence by the sheer immensity of it all. High in its grandeur, below the fog line a deep, translucent blue laced its pearly face. It emitted its own biting frost.

It wasn't just the cold that sent the shivers coursing through me sitting there in the *Blue Dolphin*. At the time it was more like the *Red Dolphin*. I saw blood where bodies weren't. There were two wooden paddles, the hakipik, a long metal hook, two gas containers, and about sixty seals. I thought of fifty bullets and how quick they'd be spent if we found ourselves, sometime tomorrow or the next day, in the midst of a herd of old aggressive harps like those we had put the hand of death mercilessly to. Would any of them remember us? I tried not to let play images of Randy and me back to back on the heaving ice alive with aroused, aggressive animals, increasing in number as we grew weary and tired. Shifting again from the brunt of the penetrating, stiffening wind, I remembered hearing of the words of one sealer to his comrades during their perishing days and endless nights on floes just like these (and really, as the gull flies, not that far from us), "Ya got ta ke'p movin'!" Aiming the rifle into the fog, away from the berg, I fired off three shots. Each one echoed off the face of the colossus and was immediately swallowed by the gloom and doom. A minute later it was just like I had never fired at all. The sea licked and the berg slicked.

This was not a nice spot, in the lee of a mountain of ice in an open boat in a tightening pack. We didn't stand a chance here. It was best we use what gas we had left to punch as far away from here as we could. No pan to crawl up on; no fires to warm us. Putting another three rounds in, I emptied the magazine into the dreariness. Then we waited with forty-four rounds, about a gallon of gasoline and a pool of hope for an early rescue that waned as fast as the light of day.

We could hear for about a mile. The tide drove us towards the berg and Randy was about to start the engine, when he exclaimed, "There!" pointing off to starboard at the welcome sound of three muffled rifle reports. Confirming the direction with me, he fired the engine to life and we cruised toward the sound. Randy chose a direct route between two large sheets that shifted together and moved apart in the swells. Having misjudged the timing, we were smack in the middle when they came together. I watched horrified as the gunnels of the boat were squeezed together and the speedboat was slowly lifted out of the water. I saw Randy hold on tight to keep from being thrown in the sea, at the same time I heard the sickening sound of timbers cracking.

As if in slow motion, the swell slipped under and the pressure eased. The edge of the sheet on the starboard side hooked into the gunnel and almost tipped us over. A rush of slobby water surged in. The pile of corpses shifted. As I threw myself to the port side, the ugly ice edge that held us broke off and a chunk big enough to ice down twenty carcasses stayed in the boat. When we rolled the other way, Randy regained control and gunned the engine to escape the next crushing blow. Both of us were very much relieved and thankful not to be in the sea.

Away from the danger, I rolled the large chunk overboard and inspected the boat for damage. Everything was dripping with blood and gore so I saw nothing. Then out of the gloom and mist came the ghost of our "mother ship."

"There she is!" I exclaimed, very excited and relieved. "My own sleeping bag tonight. Yahoo!"

"Thank God!" Randy replied, "My prayers are answered."

Relieved faces greeted us at the rail. Everyone was worried about us being out in the fog and Paul eagerly caught the painter and tied us fast. Letting out a sigh of relief, I said, "It's good to see you all again."

"We thought you had quit and gone home," Paul joked.

"I thought we were out for the night. Shocking thing to be out there without a compass."

"I had an idea of where you were," Perry stated. "How many did you get?"

"Over fifty," Randy replied, "and we got damage done to the speedboat. Two large sheets came together on us and I think there's a few timbers cracked."

"Get them unloaded, lift in the boat as quick as ya can, boys," he said. "I don't like being so close to that berg." We set about it. Darrell tossed the hawser down and Randy and I looped the steel slips over the rear flippers. When all went right, eight young harps went not so gracefully over the rail. Sometimes, because my right hand bothered me so much, I'd lose my hold before the whipline pulled the slips tight and two or three would go up empty. This was revolting work. Finally the last hawser of five went in over the rail. The *Blue Dolphin* filled the last bit of empty space; dead seals were everywhere else. Perry gunned the throttle full ahead. Sitting on the rail, I watched "Berg Colosses," who gave us quiet water to hear fall away astern. I was some glad. I reached to put up my hood to stop the pang of cold I felt starting at the roots of the steel wire on the back of my neck. From there they transformed into shoulder-squeezing shivers. My hood was already up.

We added fifty-eight to the pile of forty. In our absence, with David and Darrell out of commission, no sculping had been done. Paul and Gerard had been kept busy repairing the ship and retrieving.

I was weary, cold, and hungry. My hand throbbed and pained each time I touched it. Despite the aches, pains, and the dreariness I felt, even taking into account the pile of dead that stared at me from all about, it was good to be standing again in the gore. And besides that, there was but a single hour of the Greatest Hunt in the

World left to prosecute. The first thing I needed was a warming. Stiffly shedding my blubber clothes, I made my way to the glorious heat of the roaring engine room and found comfort for a few short moments, cradling the "hot-water-jacket." The lurching of the hull drove me away and cautiously I stripped off my damp, cold, inside clothing. Inspection of my right hand told me the poison was spreading and the swelling was increasing. The sore on my palm was coated with blood and grease, making it appear to my sore eyes like a festering boil. I felt pain shooting to my elbow and I made haste to the washroom to clean myself up.

My hand gave me a great deal of concern and the thought of a hundred seals, waiting to be pelted, made me moan in the mirror. There was only Randy, Paul, Gerard and me left to do the work. Perry didn't pitch in and up to now, Rodney did nothing, other than steer. If I dropped out, three men had to do it all. I decided to say nothing and work on the best I could. The Hunt was over and it wouldn't be long before I'd have medical attention. Another day wouldn't kill me.

I had no appetite but I ate a tin of hot beans and some bread. Food was getting scarce. David had the last turkey thawing in the sink. Tomorrow we were going to eat it, along with the last of the vegetables. As hungry as I was, I didn't relish the thought. The thought of what was waiting on deck killed my taste buds.

It was not a nice evening in the floes. Rain, drizzle and fog, lashed on a thirty-five-knot wind. Not fit for an old bitch hood to pup, but Perry would not put away the rifle. He endured the elements all for that one last kill, as if one more would make everything all right; like a demon in frantic pursuit of the golden "seal" of approval. Just before closing time, he brought the final curtain down on one more lounging young harp.

I was bent over, disemboweling a steaming carcass, concentrating on keeping my balance while my bad hand worked the blade, when I felt the dragger slow. Straightening up my breaking back to toss the steaming organs into the sea, I looked around. So this is how my final Hunt would end. *Bang!*

"Over the side, Mickey," Gerard said.

Perry was passing the rifles down to Rodney when I climbed back in over the rail for the last time. "I guess that's it then," he said, stepping down from the hatch. "How many did we get?"

"About 220," Gerard answered.

"That's about 1,200 all totalled?" Shaking his head, he followed Rodney inside the warm superstructure, turning on the spar-lights, leaving us to take care of the fat.

Gerard noticed I had a bad hand. "What have you gone and done?" he asked.

I told him what happened.

"Let's see."

Pulling off my bloody glove, I showed him my swollen hand. He seemed shocked. "Seal's finger!" he exclaimed. "That's dangerous. An old fellow home lost his hand to that. You got to keep that clean. Have ya showed it to Perry?"

"No, I haven't showed it to him. I figure I'll get it checked on as soon as we get in."

"We're not going in yet. Perry is going to stay out for as long as the water and grub lasts and hunt old hoods. The quota is still open for them."

That statement sent a pang of dread right through me. "Well, I'll work away for as long as I can, then I'll tell him," I replied, pulling the bloody glove back over my hand and painfully grasping the knife with it, bending again to finish my sculp.

Once, at 10:30, Perry poked his head out the galley window to survey the work. He was only there watching for a couple of minutes before he withdrew his head out of the cold and tightly closed the window.

We all worked like slaves in the misery. David did what he could with his bad back and Darrell hardly stopped using his one good hand. Gerard started singing an old Newfoundland folk song about the sea and soon we were all singing along. It was a little bit of cheer amid a deck full of gore. *Wave over wave, sea over bow. I'm as happy a man as the sea will allow....*

"How foolish am I to be at this," Randy stated, tossing a twitching body toward the block for decapitation and "de-flipperization." It landed with a splat atop the pile and slithered in the gore. We were concentrating on getting them all pelted first; chopping, washing, scrubbing and stowing came later. My office was quite a mess. Most everything was covered with dead seals, seal parts, or seal pelts. Some pelts were lying grease up, others grease down. Some of them blocked the drain-ports in the gunnels, restricting the free flow of slobby-red fluids off the deck. The action of the ship rolling in the swells caused the gallons and gallons of blood to slosh from one side to the other in frantic waves that at times crested halfway up my blubber boot. I tried really hard not to look at it, but you can't pelt with your eyes closed.

"We're all foolish to be here," David replied, holding a hideous clump of dripping entrails in his hand. "Anybody want to buy a perfectly good heart?" Holding the grisly mass by the heart, he used his knife to cut the rest away. It landed in the slosh with a splash.

"I know that's true," Randy responded, positioning a fresh one belly-up between his feet. "But I got to be the foolishest. Perry told me that if I wanted, I could have taken this trip off."

"What!" David exclaimed. "You could be home snuggled up to your wife tonight and you chose to be here! My son, you needs your head checked. You're cracked!" Bending again, he reached a bloody hand for the flipper. "By Jesus, if he had to tell me that, I knows where I'd be to tonight and it wouldn't be here in this cauldron of filth breaking my back for nothing!"

"Yes," Randy lamented bending down with his blade, "How foolish I am, boys, oh boys, oh boys."

I was working in the filth on the starboard side when the hull slipped out from under my slimy boots. The tilt in the deck threw me against the rail. "Watch out!" In the naked glare of the mast lights I looked to see the heap of harps sliding towards me. Unable to move, afraid to lift my feet for fear of getting tossed over the low railing that came to just above the backs of my knees, I braced myself for the impact. The dead weight pinned my legs against the gunnel and my upper body whiplashed way out over the rail. I thought I was gone. Only the weight of the seals kept me on deck. After the ship threw back the other way, I dug my way out of the heap, careful not to pull off my boot. Darrell told me I had reminded him of a bronco-buster.

Midnight saw us washing down the last of the pelts and meat and the speedboat. An inspection of the timbers showed three ribs cracked on the port side, four on the other. The *Blue Dolphin* was damaged beyond further use. Perry came out for his inspection and wasn't too well pleased. "We won't be using her for the hoods, anyway," he said, before going back inside. "Too bad that had to happen. That's a loss, that is." He was not a nice man, I decided.

I don't know where I got the energy to crawl into my coffin. Every part of my body was shrunken with the frost, aching, paining and complaining. I ate very little for lunch. My bad hand throbbed up to my bicep, the veins in my forearm were inflamed to my elbow, and from the gauntness of my face, I knew I had lost at least ten pounds. When I held my hand against my chest, the throbbing seemed to ease a little. I decided that I would tell the captain about it tomorrow.

I shuddered at the thought of staying out to kill hoods. They were scarce and mostly solitary, which meant to kill fifty was a good day. That translated into hours and hours on end, standing around freezing, in the open. Most of the ports on the northeast coast were choked with drift ice and the likeliest port to discharge was St. John's.

Everyone seemed to be glad it was over. Seals were scarce and the weather was deplorable. It was too bad we hadn't got a load. As it stood now, we were going to make very little from the work we had done, the beating we had received and the chances we had taken. Literally, not enough for a good cleaning-up. Another hundred, in three or four more days of misery, wasn't going to make the trip for us. "The Hunt is over, let's get the hell in out of it," we thought but we weren't the man in control. He was in the wheel-house listening to the radio: "Security. Security. Security. Marine weather forecast...Funk Island Bank...strong Northerlies, thirty-five to forty knots…snow flurries…lows minus two….”

“Oh God! I don’t want to hear that!” I quietly wailed to myself at the thought of the upcoming day. Racked with pain, torn by strain, exhausted, tormented, sore and “low-minded,” I lay searching for rest, while the cradle rocked in loose drift ice, fourteen hours’ steam from St. John’s.

Just a few minutes later, it seemed, the captain’s voice entered the forecastle. “Boys, put down the fat.”

I hoped it was a dream. “Put down the fat!” Paul echoed. “It’s four in the morning! Christ, we’ve only had four hours’ rest!”

“Come on, let’s get it done,” Gerard said, switching on the light in his berth. “Once it’s done it’s done!”

“Yeah! That’ll give us more time standing around all day, beat to pieces and freezing to death.”

The glare of the light brought me awake and I groaned over to see Gerard tucking his shirt down inside his pants. With sleep in his eyes and a disgusted look on his face, he looked right at me and said, “Time to get up, Mickey.” Feeling the same way as I had when I crawled in, I found one consolation: I wasn’t out in the floes in the speedboat. Ten minutes later, I was in the freezer, under the glare of the mast-lights, ending a yawn with a shiver that contracted every sore muscle in my body. *Brrrrrr*. It was barbaric.

My hand was bad. It was difficult for me to close it to make a fist. The skin was stretched and swollen, and the puncture hole was filled with puss and was very tender. I should have notified the captain, but I guess my mind was poisoned and contaminated like the rest of me both inside and out, to the point where my thoughts were, *It’s almost over, let’s get it done.*

Our blubber clothes slobbed over as we paraded back and forth, putting down the pelts. I could only carry one, like David and Darrell. I showed the boys the reason why and when they saw it, they were surprised and shocked. “Show the skipper!”

“I will by and by.”

Next the bloody meat had to be stowed. It seemed to take forever and everyone was working like dogs. Once, during a trek back to the heap, Darrell stopped in mid-stride, turned around looking at me and said, "Will you be as glad as me when this misery is finally over?"

"Thrice as happy, Darrell," I said. Now keep moving or step out of the way to let me pass. I got to keep moving or I'll freeze!"

I received my marrow-freezing scrub-down in the gloom of the dawn, my teeth and skeleton rattling all the while. I wouldn't let them scrub my right arm. I said I'd wash it off later. Not that I really gave a good goddamn. All I cared about was the heat I had left in my sleeping bag. Darrell helped me out of my blubber clothes and told me to put iodine on my hand after I washed and cleaned it.

The captain was in the chair reading the Bible when I passed through. I stopped for a moment and looked at him but he was focused on his reading and didn't look at me. Single-handedly, I went down in the forecastle, moaned off my clothes and groaned my way in bunk. It felt like someone had beaten me with a hakapik. Lying there, I knew I should have showed the skipper. I knew it but I didn't have the energy to get up. My pillow felt good, my head was heavy and my hand wasn't bothering me that much. The tiny forecastle was quiet and my sleeping bag was warm and comfortable. I opted for sleep.

The main engine started, followed shortly by the first crash. I swore a venomous oath to myself as the first lurch drove me up against the wooden framing. The tiny room was quiet and peaceful no more.

Unwilling to forfeit my bunk, no matter what, I punched the time while the *Perry* punched the floes. I figured there was a contest going on between me and the hull to see who could endure the most. Picturing the skipper grinding his teeth as he aimed a big one at my ear made me snarl around in my tomb like a tormented wolverine in its den.

The muffled report of the rifle ousted me. I felt the boat stop and for a moment there was piece and quiet. At first I thought he had shut down for the day and a wave of relief washed over me. Then the rifle fired. Hoods. "Oh God!"

My poisoned mind told me not to be late for work, and I crawled out woefully and dressed. By the time I got on deck, an enormous "dog hood" lay bleeding out. Paul and Gerard stood over him.

"There's no need for you to be out here," Gerard said, when he saw me reaching for my greasy, stiff, blubber clothes.

"We can handle this," Paul seconded, "You go on back inside."

"I'm out here now, so I'm not going back in."

"Please yourself," Gerard replied, reaching for his steel and giving his knife a few fast rubs before he stood over the beast and with a single, continuous, nine-foot cut, slit him open from tongue to tail. Paul sculped down one side and Gerard did the other and I used the meat hook to pull away the five-hundred-pound, six-dollar, carcass. The sight of the revolting thing caused my stomach to convulse and I'm sure that if there had been anything in it, I would have donated it to the gulls.

At 9:00 A.M., number one for the day was butchered, sculped, washed, decapitated, quartered, stowed and cooling and I had made twenty cents. I had a like to die. It was an hour before the rifle sounded again. I huddled in the lee, clasping the hot pipes, the time passing like the melting of ice. *Bang!*

David was preparing dinner, Darrell was in the spar. Randy was on the top-deck with Perry and Rodney. Perry came down for a warm, looked at us through watering eyes, shook himself and said, "Up there is where it is cold." Nobody replied and he went on inside in the warm.

The smell of turkey, diesel fumes, soot and smoke on the blasts of penetrating arctic winds didn't arouse any pangs of hunger inside me. What it meant most for me was that it was midday and I'd soon get to go inside. Having spent most of the time in the engine room thawing out, I didn't spend much time eating. Perry didn't seem to notice anything but the food on his plate and he wolfed it down without raising his head. After thanking the cook, he disappeared out the door and within minutes we were scurrying to keep all the pots, pans and dishes on the table.

No one was in any hurry to finish and everyone dreaded to hear the sound of the gun. Rodney followed his father topside, leaving us with the dishes. Rodney and Paul cleaned them while Gerard and I swept and cleaned the floors of the galley, the wheel-house, the hallway, washroom and forecastle. Looking out at the shifting ice, wind and rain, I was contented to wash anything inside; anything was better than being out there.

At two o'clock, it was too miserable for even Perry to endure it and he shut down the main engine. Before he got settled in his chair, we were all in our bunks. "Get sleep while you can aboard this one," Darrell said, crawling in his berth.

I heard Perry, in the wheel-house, mumbling something about "being in bed in the middle of the day," but the sound of ice gnawing at the hull drowned him out. I didn't care anyway. St. John's would not come quickly enough for me.

Only a short spell after that, Randy clambered out over me to make his first trip to the washroom. "I got a bad stomach," he groaned. Within the next hour, he got out six times; each time he returned he looked a year older. "I'm not very good," he stammered, "It must be the turkey. I told David he shouldn't keep that out overnight."

"None of us are sick," Gerard said.

"Everyone reacts different ways to different things," he replied, standing, holding onto the ladder with one hand, rubbing his stomach with the other, unsure whether to run up or crawl in. "I'm poisoned," he concluded.

"Poisoned! Poisoned!" Darrell echoed. "You're not the only one that's poisoned! We're all poisoned with this racket! Who wouldn't be poisoned? I hope we don't see another bloody hood!" No one contradicted him. Randy groaned and disappeared up the ladder.

Randy was bed-ridden with food poisoning, David was broken across the back, Darrell was down to one hand and I had the use of only one arm. The food supply was dwindling and the water was getting down to drastic levels that saw us denied our weekly shower. According to Gerard we had fuel enough for another week and we could have another change of underwear at any time. No one laughed. As far as Perry was concerned, we could survive for that long eating seal meat. He wanted every single one he could get and I had a feeling that it wasn't for our benefit that he prolonged the abuse. I decided to ignore the swelling and throbbing for another while. I didn't want the Hunt ended because of me. I was reminded of a plaque our family had given our seafaring father. It read, "It's a swell ship for the skipper but it's a 'hell-ship' for the crew." How fitting.

At five o'clock, Perry considered it to be fit enough to continue the assault and we got the message in the form of a tremendous shock to the cabin that shook and jolted everything from stem to stern, mast head to keel. Gerard disappeared up the ladder, followed closely by Paul, swearing, pulling on his clothes and holding on, all at the same time.

By the time I got suited, two large hoods, a large dog and a female, were bleeding up the deck. Both Paul and Gerard told me to go inside but I refused. Before long the two of them were cooling on the stern and I had taken up position at the hydraulic lines. It was a rotten day in the shifting floes: four-metre swells, biting winds at gusts to forty knots. The driving rain and slop-snow stuck to my suit. Looking at the crew, I knew they were in misery too. The seconds dripped off the iceberg of time.

At 7:00 p.m., in the driving sleet, Rodney and Paul roped a large pan and Perry passed the guns and ammo down from atop the wheel-house. The long, punishing day had netted us eight hoods: one dollar and sixty cents. At that point in time I didn't care. All I wanted was the warmth of my sleeping bag and a good night's sleep. My arm throbbed past my elbow and it bothered me very much to move it. I sensed Perry saw I was injured but he didn't mentioned it. I thought to show my infected hand to him when I was passing through on my way to the forecastle, but decided not to. He was curled up in his chair, reading the Bible, the radio blasting out gospel music. I went on to bed.

The sleeping bag was comfortable and soon the shivering had diminished to sporadic uncontrollable shakes coming three or four times a minute, lasting about ten seconds. *Thump!* The hull shuddered from the shock, and realizing sleep was going to be a scarce commodity, I lay back in bed thinking about it all. It wasn't worth it. No amount of money could compensate for the way I felt. Between the thumps and bangs, the painful shifts and turns, I sought to find rest and comfort in a sea of misery, thirteen hours' steam from the Health Science Centre in St. John's. *Thump!*

"Security, Security, Security. Marine forecast issued by...for Sunday...gale force Easterlies...forty...fifty-five...rain, drizzle, and fog...." *Oh God! Will this nightmare ever end?*

SUNDAY, APRIL 20

The elements didn't matter to the skipper huddled in the heated control booth at 6:00 A.M. the next morning when he drove us with full force into the floes. Gerard scampered out and turned on the glaring cabin light. I groaned and shifted to hold on with my good hand. Before going up the ladder, he touched my shoulder and said, "You stay in bed. There's no need of you on deck, yet."

Paul was the next to scurry from his berth, and he told me the same thing. "Don't be so foolish. Stay in bunk."

Darrell clamoured out next and battled into his clothes, favouring his injury. "We can handle this. Don't you get up!"

David made no motion to get up. Randy scurried out, not bothering to pull on anything. He darted up the ladder saying, "I hope no one is in the bathroom!"

Lying there in the glare, I knew I had to get up. It wasn't just the physical beating. I felt I was letting the crew down by staying in. The thought of the sweat from the engine room freezing on my back and chest while I battled on those stiff blubber clothes made me pull the covers up over my bony shoulders. I couldn't remember dreading a dawning more.

A few collisions later Randy came down and crawled back in his bunk. "I'm some sick," he said, "too sick to be out there."

"So am I."

"Then don't go out. That seal-finger is serious stuff. If that gets to your heart you're dead." The ship stopped. "Number one for the day, dead ahead," he said.

I could picture what was going on out there. From atop the wheelhouse, Perry was bent at the gunning table, focusing through the wind and drizzle on the skull of this large hood. Rodney was at the controls and Paul was standing by the rail, waiting like a retriever for the shot. Darrell and Gerard were waiting as well. *Bang! Bang! Bang!* The hull crashed forward. In my mind, I saw the black cloud of soot and oil.

The hull stopped again and I used the dead-time to squirm out and get dressed. Randy rolled over towards me and asked to see my hand. "My God, that don't look good to me!"

"It don't look to good to me, either." It was swollen and the skin was tight and red. The wound was enlarged and enflamed. I couldn't make a fist.

"Show the skipper. He'll get a chopper sent out to pick you up. That's what Search and Rescue is for."

"No choppers this weather. Only hoods and fools out in this."

"If you don't feel like telling Perry, tell Rodney. He's sure to tell him. He tells him everything else."

Gingerly pulling my shirt on over my sore arm, I was up the ladder and in the washroom before the next collision moved everything aboard. I wasn't the least bit hungry but I knew that I should eat so I toasted the last piece of homemade bread, chewed it up really good and drank a cup of tea. After it all was down, it lay there in my shrunken stomach, primed to come back up at the first smell of smoke or the first whiff of pungent "belly" steam.

My head throbbed in unison with the Volvo as I dressed in the engine room. The smell of bilge water and diesel fumes mixed with blubber nauseated me and it took a lot longer to battle into the stinking clothes. I was glad the sleeves were cut away because I didn't think my swollen hand would pass through. As I wrestled into my heavy shirt, my sunglasses fell out. Picking them up, I put them away… not today! Twice the hull lurched and I used my bad hand to catch myself. Both times I swore away to the engine while I waited in the suffocating heat and noise and stench for the floes to give me a chance to grab my hat, scarf, gloves, vest, and coat to escape up the ladder. I was all in by the time I cleared the hatch. The crew told me how foolish I was to be up. I knew they were right but I wanted to see it through to the end and decided to write this story when I had got the hell out of this God-forsaken place.

"Proper thing! Let them know what goes on out here." Paul said, standing up beside me and helping me put on my greasy, brittle blubber clothes. The feel of the material in my bare hands was the worst part of it all.

I didn't do much. Clinging to the hot pipes, I watched the drizzle in the wind over the shifting pack. The warmth from the pipes seemed to ease the throbbing in my right arm and it heated my core and kept my veins from slobbing up. Around 9:00 A.M. we had four hoods cooling.

Perry came down for his warm and hastily went inside. I decided to stop him on his way out and show him my hand. I didn't care if I never saw another bloody one.

Twenty minutes later he did come out but before I could get my body slued around, he was gone up the ladder. Not having the energy to climb, I decided to tell him the next time.

The ship stopped. Looking along the hull into the bite of the wind, I spotted a big fish-eater lying alone one hundred yards away. We rose and fell and rolled in the swells and he rose and fell, three swells over. It took a while for the rifle to fire and as I watched the bloody thing, I thought to myself, "Get in the water, you stupid low life!"

Bang! The high-powered rifle fired and the gigantic head dropped and lay still. For an instant, I envied him. He had it over, but I still had it to endure. "Another twenty cents," Paul said sarcastically, choosing a gaff. "We're into the big bucks, now." A cloud of smoke and soot engulfed us and I almost lost my breakfast. Soon the winch strained to bring him onboard and the repulsive sight was before my eyes. Promptly, as the long-liner surged forward with a crash, Gerard split him from lip to tail with one slash. The intestines spilled out on deck. Paul kicked them with his boot and took up position on the other side while Darrell, single-handedly, used the hook. Standing there watching, I could do nothing to help.

Rodney came down for his warm some time later. We were in the huddle in the lun, Darrell was warming his hands on the hot lines. As Rodney passed by us, Paul spoke up saying, "Mick, show Rodney your hand."

Pulling off my contaminated, woollen glove, I put my swelled hand up in his face and turned it over. "Oh my!" he said.

"Oh my," is right, I echoed, "I punctured it last week with a strand of steel cable and its got worse ever since. Right now, stabs of pain are shooting right to my armpits." While I spoke I looked him in the eye and for some reason I thought he was going to say, "That's serious. I'll tell father right away and we'll get you to the hospital. You go in and lie down."

Instead, he looked back at me with his eyes watering and replied, "Mick, it looks to me like you got an 'in-fact-ion'!" Before my poisoned mind registered what I thought was a snicker, he disappeared inside, closing the door firmly behind him.

"What do you think of that, now," Darrell asked no one in particular.

"It's hard to know what to think of that," Paul stated and spit on the deck. I didn't say anything. Darrell moved away and I grabbed hold of the pipes. I didn't know what to think. My head throbbed like my arm and I just fixed my stare on the foggy ice floes. My mind seemed to freeze like everything else.

Perry came down for his warms and munches off and on but he didn't make any mention to me and I didn't make mention to him. I figured he must know; the man wasn't blind. He could see well enough to put the bullets in the hoods, so for sure he could see a man dying on deck. If he didn't care, why should I? "Maybe he'll mention it when he comes out" I thought hopefully to myself.

He didn't mention it all day but sometimes, when I was single-handedly dragging the steaming carcasses and piling them in the stern, I'd look up to see him standing in the steering booth, scanning with spy-glasses. He'd frequently turn to scan the deck to see me there battling with the meat, flavouring my right hand, as best I could. I'd look back at him and see him grin or sneer, then turn back, lifting the glasses to his eyes. I knew he knew.

During one of his frequent trips to the washroom, Randy poked his head out through the window and informed everyone that there was no water left. When Darrell shouted the news to Perry, he made no reply. "We'll soon have to get in out of this," I thought.

With no water to wash in, I climbed in as I came off deck. I really didn't care. Fourteen hours of misery had netted us twelve seals. All I wanted was to feel the sleeping bag around me, to feel the soft pillow surround my aching head and to lay my throbbing hand upon my chest next to my cheek. I was thankful for one thing as I climbed in my tomb; the relentless pounding all day had resulted in our finding a quiet harbour. The tiny room was peaceful and still. The nibbling of the ice didn't bother me at all and I succumbed quickly.

Monday, April 21

5:30 A.M. arrived with a bang that violently shook the forecastle and jolted awake everyone lying inside. Gerard scrambled out, hastily dressed and scurried up. Paul climbed out after him and followed suit. Darrell failed to respond to the wake-up call. Regretfully, I pushed back the covers and carefully groaned my way out.

Wind, fog, and the sleet were in abundance. The pipes were hot and the bit of heat revived me while I watched the crew do the work. I did help drag the meat and pelts and drop them down in the hold. Paul and Darrell stowed them away. There weren't many and it didn't take long.

Perry came down for his warm around 10:00 A.M. and I stopped him before he disappeared inside, saying, " Skipper, I got something to show you."

"What's that, boy?" he asked.

Taking off my clean glove, I showed him my swollen and distorted hand and informed him that the pain was shooting to my armpit.

"You should take care of that. There's no need for you to be on deck. Go in and scald it in salty water."

I went to the washroom and washed my hand and cleaned it up as best I could with water from the barrel, and applied some iodine. Perry was in his chair when I came out and I made it a point to show him the streaks of blue that travelled up my arm to my armpit.

"Rodney got some pills there, if you want to take them," he said.

"I don't feel like taking someone else's pills. I'll get my own prescription when I get to the doctor."

"That's up to you," he replied. "In the meantime, keep it elevated. It will bother you less and keep the swelling down."

I went below to "sick-bay" with David, nursing a bad back, and Randy, getting over his bout of food poisoning. We must have looked like a pitiful crew. There was no rest to be found, but there was warmth and anything was better than being out there. To my surprise, I didn't feel one bit bad at all, just sore, sick and tired and my head hurt like all hell.

Lying there taking the beating, I was conscious of the ongoing Hunt. The crashing and banging would stop abruptly and all would be peaceful. Then the rifle would fire and the hull would pounce. Perry was relentless in his pursuit of every hood he could find riding the floes. I thought of Paul and Darrell and Gerard and I felt bad.

By noon, the smell of blubber off my body drove me out to the open deck door. Perry came down for a warm and as he passed me by, and said, "You're not very good."

"No sir, I'm not," I said with a shiver, as a blast of wind shot down my back. "I have seen better days."

He went back outside and called up to Rodney to bring down the guns. "I'm setting course for St. John's."

That was the best news I had heard in a long time and it gave me the energy to crawl back into my berth. This time when the pans struck, I welcomed the sound and feel of it. The hull seemed to say, "Get out of my way. I've got to get a dying man to hospital!" I spent the time before we made the open sea wondering if each one was going to be the last.

I passed out while I counted and awoke to the sound of water whooshing past my ear. The tiny room gently rolled back and forth, rose and dipped on the swells, fluidly and noiselessly. The continuous throb of the engine sent a sense of reassurance through me and I was lifted by the thought that St. John's was getting closer by the roll.

The next time I woke it was dark, and I heard Perry calling the harbour-master in St. John's, informing him that we were three miles off. Two tractor-trailers were waiting at Pier 17 to take our cargo.

Everyone got up to see the city lights.

In the wheel-house with all the crew, rocked by the last of the ocean swells, we passed through "the Narrows" and disturbed the calm waters of the harbour. Off-loading was the topic of discussion. "I can't go down in the hold," I said, when Darrell asked who was going down there. I hoped Perry was going to say, "No, you are going straight to the hospital," but he didn't. Instead he said, "You can man the hook."

Before I knew it, my reply was out, "Okay. I'll man the hook." The fog and mist looked soft and inviting first when I went out to prepare for tying up, but before I got my blubber pants on, I knew the lights, as plentiful as they were, gave no warmth. I didn't bother putting on my blubber-jacket; it was too stiff for me to bend, too repulsive to touch and I knew it would kill me to pull the sleeve over my sore arm. My heavy winter's coat was destined for the dump anyway, so another eight hours in the fat, grease and blood wasn't going to hurt it.

I did very little to help the crew make fast to the pier. I just stood back and watched them do their work. Climbing onto the dock, I had an urge to run to Water Street, hail the first car and get someone to take me to the hospital. Instead, my poisoned mind told me to stay and endure it to the end. Another eight hours wouldn't kill me. "You man the hook."

At 11:00 P.M., in the rain, wind and fog, the first sling of ten pelts was plucked up and loaded into the large plastic container on the dock. Paul and Darrell were in the hold strapping them on and Randy and David were on the dock, pulling the boom and pelts over, unhooking them after they landed in the tub. Gerard worked the winch beside me and Rodney kept tally. Perry was inside cleaning himself up. The water tanks were filling up and there was water in abundance. The thought of a long, hot shower comforted me as I pulled the boom and hook back. I'd hold on to it until Darrell called out, "Hook!," then I'd lower it down to him.

When a pound was emptied, David and Rodney changed places. I made the comment that it was the first time I had seen Rodney do anything other than steer. I also realized that I had not seen him make a jump, pelt a seal, nor wash a dish. I wasn't all that careful with the hook and a couple of times struck him on the shoulder. "Watch what you're doing with that hook!" he'd roar up at me. I ignored him.

Tuesday, April 22

In the galley I could hear the hockey game playing and off and on. Perry would slide back the glass and look out to see us working the fat. I'd wait in the lee of the superstructure to lower the hook, holding my bad arm across my chest, feeling like death warmed over. He'd stare at the deck for a long time saying nothing, looking fresh and clean but with a disappointed air about him. He never asked how I was. He didn't care. I guessed all he thought about was all the seals he didn't get. "How much is left aboard, Gerard?"

At 2:00 A.M. the last sling of pelts was hoisted out into the blowing rain. The ship was unloaded in such a way that the hull tilted toward the dock to enable the lift to be pulled over easily. The slippery, tilted deck caused me misery. I'd slip and slide and stumble like a drunken man, trying to do a two-handed job with one. If I stood up at the edge of the hatch and let go of the lip, gravity slid me right to the rail. It was a constant battle and each time I used my bad hand, I paid dearly for it.

Perry had his last look for the night after the hockey game was over. The first net-bag filled with blood-dripping carcasses came out of the hold. "How much is left on, Rodney?" He was there for a long while watching me battle my way back to the hatch, cradling the bloody net-bag in my arms and tossing it down in the hold. I wondered what he was thinking about as he lingered there staring. I knew what he wasn't thinking about.

A scallop dragger was off-loading further up the pier, astern.

Around 3:00 A.M. a group of five crew members soaked up to where we were off-loading. We learned that they had eighty thousand pounds. At $2.80 a pound, that was a lot of money. One also told us of a five-day storm they encountered two hundred miles out in the "blue drop." Crew sleeping quarters were forward on the dragger, he told us, while the net-bag of black, blood-dripping carcasses rose between us. The galley was astern and for the duration of the storm no one had eaten. No one would leave to cross the wave-swept deck.

"How much is that worth an hour?" I asked him, holding the filthy dripping netbag to the chest of my once blue, good winter coat.

Looking at me he cocked his head for a moment in thought before replying, "A lot more than $2.80 a pound."

"We'll 'swamp' you a meal of fresh flippers for a meal of scallops," I suggested. He looked for a time while the fifthy net-bag passed between us again. Pointing at the dripping flesh, he shook his head from side to side, "No thank you," he replied.

"I don't blame you," I responded.

It was 6:30 A.M. and the lights of the city were losing their luster when the last revolting bag of black meat landed in the tub and I battled back the gruesome net-bag, for what I knew would be the last time in my miserable life. I was too tired to even wash and I left my filthy coat with my filthy blubber pants. It was all destined for the garbage. As I crawled in my bunk, my last thoughts were of a long, hot shower, and a call to my sister, Maureen, first thing in the morning. The misery was almost over.

At 8:00 A.M. I got up on my own. No ice-pans banged to get in. With a fistful of clean clothes, I made directly for the shower. Perry was in his chair, reading, when I finished washing and cleaning myself. I wasn't feeling very good even after the invigorating wash.

"What are your plans?" he asked.

I wasn't wearing a shirt. Lifting my arm up in the air, I again showed him my distorted hand and the blue streaks and replied, "I'm going ashore now to phone my sister and get her to take me to the hospital."

"You can use the ship's phone, if you want."

"No, I'm going to walk up to the store. The walk will do me good."

Maureen was home but she did not have a car available. She was concerned about me and suggested I call a cab and go directly to the hospital. Although I insisted I was "not that bad," she said she'd be down to Pier 17 to get me at dinner time. Returning aboard to wait, I informed the skipper of my plans and went below to pack my bags.

Maureen was shocked when I showed her my arm and she insisted on taking me to the doctor right away. At 1:00 P.M. a nurse summoned me to the examination room at the Health Science Complex. After I was seated, she stuck a thermometer under my tongue, examined my arm and took my blood pressure. She seemed concerned and told me it was very serious.

The examining doctor asked, "Headache?"

"Massive."

"Appetite?"

"None."

He ordered that X-rays be taken of the wound and told me that I was to be admitted for three days to receive IV treatment. "This is very serious. You should have come to the hospital promptly after arriving in port."

"I know," I replied. I told him I had plans to go home that evening and asked him if it would be all right if I received the treatment at Grand Falls hospital. Reluctantly, he agreed, on the condition that I take a treatment of IV before leaving and report to my family doctor first thing in the morning. I readily agreed and sat quietly absorbing the bag of antibiotic. Drip…drip…drip.

It was 6:00 P.M. before the doctor had finished making a plaster protector-shield for my bad hand. He told me to keep it elevated in the sling he gave me to wear around my neck. He also gave me a prescription and a letter to give to my family doctor first thing in the morning. Reassuring him that I would, I thanked him and left the hospital, nursing a severe case of cellulitis.

Wednesday, April 23

At 1:00 A.M. I crawled into my own bed on solid ground. My family was alarmed and concerned for me. After two baths and a shower, I slipped between the sheets all fresh and clean, relieved and exhausted and almost too tired to raise a smile. No ice banged to get in. The misery was over. Thank God.

The doctor drew back in alarm when he saw my arm the next morning. He immediately referred me to the Central Newfoundland Hospital for IV treatment.

Before being shown to my bed, a nurse informed me that the wound had to be lanced. Leading me to an operating room, she instructed me to get up on the table. As I did, it reminded me of crawling into my tomb, only here it was very bright and spacious. Pulling a side board out from the table, she placed my hand down on the surface and cleaned the wound. The surgeon came in and sat down beside my extended arm, with his big back to me.

"This is going to hurt for a minute," the nurse said, "you can move anything but your right arm."

During the course of that agonizing minute, as the doctor cut deep into my hand, I broke out in a wash of sweat. I flailed my left arm about, kicked the air with both my feet and grinded my teeth, but I didn't move my right hand. The thought of how a seal must feel, if it was not dead when I slit it open from tongue to tail, crossed my mind. I squirmed in misery on the table. It ended when the surgeon pressed down firmly and the pressure was relieved.

And so was I. Sitting up, I took a deep breath and expelled a great sigh of relief. My blood was spattered all over the floor. "Thanks, Doc."

"You did good," he said.

"I wimped out," I replied, wiping away the sweat that streamed down my face, "but I do feel better."

Three days and twenty-seven bags of IV later, I was released back to the care of my family doctor and the misery of the Hunt was behind me. The swelling went down, the dead skin flaked away, and the blue streaks up my arm faded and disappeared. I find that I have an ever-increasing desire to lounge about on ice-pans when it's sunny and from time to time I have a craving for raw fish. Other than that, I'll soon be back to "abnormal."

I'll never do it again. As for tradition, to hell with that. I know next spring when the seals come, I won't be there to meet them. If I ever get the urge to hunt seals again, I'll read a small portion of this account and remember the agonies, miseries, hardships, dangers and the backbreaking, repulsive, disgusting, grisly work. I'll lie down until the urge passes. I'll think of the crew that saw me endure my miseries and relieved me of quite a few. I'll picture them huddled on the exposed deck of the lurching long-liner, waiting for the report of the rifle. Never again will I make 150 sorties in a single day and never again will I hear those dreaded words, "Over the side, Mickey."